Made
Plain

STANLEY LOVE TATE III

For those with more month than money —

CONTENTS

Part III – Money

DISCLAIMER
YOU'RE NOT MY CLIENT. YET

I'm an attorney. You know this. I know this.

So let's get clear about some things, right now. Just because you bought this book doesn't mean I've somehow become your attorney. And just because I wrote this book doesn't mean that I'm advertising my services. As you'll see, I'm not advising you to do anything and I'm not trying to sell you anything. I'm just providing information. That's it.

Consult an attorney or other student loan professional for advice and guidance.

I did my best to make sure that the information I provided within these pages is accurate. But student loan law (like most any other law) is always changing. So if you notice that something's inaccurate, contact me. I'll fix it in the next edition.

Also, you'll notice there are links in this book. If you follow those links (most links go to Reddit and You Tube) you'll go to a third party website. I can't vouch for the information on that site. And I can't guarantee that by going there your device won't end up with a virus or some other issue. So if you want, skip the links entirely.

Finally, you will come across a few cuss words. I count less than 10 in over 20 thousand words. Not that many. But still the cussing's there. Why do I cuss? To take advantage — for the right reasons — of the little extra creative leeway that comes with controlling the publishing. Besides, sometimes dropping an F—bomb just feels right, don't you think?

WHY I WROTE THIS BOOK

You. I wrote this book for you. For my friends. For my colleagues. For everyone I know that has no clue what to do with their student loans despite information being everywhere like ScarJo at the end of *Lucy*.

Student loan information is everywhere but it's not in one place that's easy to scan, easy to grasp, and with enough detail to be helpful but not so much detail that it's burdensome.

Trying and failing to find that place is what got me interested in writing this book.

But before I decided I would write this book, I read damn never every blog, online article, book, e-book, white paper, law review article, and treatise I could find on student loans. And here's what my reading revealed: the authors who tried to summarize student loan law seemed more caught up on selling themselves than they did on giving you enough information to help you develop your repayment strategy. And the authors who did give you enough information, either presented it in a cumbersome manner or gave you too much damn information.

No one wants to struggle to find what they need. And few people care enough about student loans to want to learn it on a granular level. I assume that most of you are like me and want to know enough to find a solution that makes sense; to find a solution that lets you live comfortably while repaying student loans quickly.

Those two assumptions led me to put pen to paper.

I hope you read this book and find all the information you need to develop your student loan strategy in one place. I hope you find that that place (this book) presents the information in a way that's easy to scan and easy to grasp and that it gives you enough detail to be helpful but not so much detail that it's burdensome.

I encourage you to email me at tate@tateesq.com or call me at 314.499.8177 and tell me if you believed I did or didn't do what I set out to do. And if you want, write a review on Amazon telling others about my performance.

Whether your comments come in the form of criticism or acclaim, your comments matter. They will make the next edition that much better.

Best.

I designed this book with the idea that no one would read it cover to cover. You're looking for answers. You're not trying to become a student loan expert. (If you are, read Student Loan Law by the National Consumer Law Center.) So I designed the book for you to jump to the section that best answers your questions.

The book is divided into three major sections: federal student loans, private student loans, and money. The federal and private student loan sections discuss repayment, forgiveness, default (and its consequences) and forgiveness. The money section discusses 13 tips on paying your loans, establishing a budget, and understanding how your student loans affect your credit report and score.

I hope you enjoy. I hope you get your answers.

As Kobe told Kanye, "You're welcome."

INTRODUCTION

How about instead of writing this introduction I just share John Oliver's 16 plus minute take down of student loan debt (http://bit.ly/1rtpa4L)?

No? You demand an introduction?

Cool. Let me be brief.

Student loan debt is a problem. And it's a problem that's only getting worse.

In your search for student loan help, you will come across people or materials promising to reveal tricks and secrets to getting rid of your loans quickly. To quote Huey Freeman, "That's some ol' bullshit."

There ain't no magic pill. No button. No secret. No nothing that will get rid of your loans immediately.

There are plenty of things you can do, however, to plan an effective strategy to deal with your loans. And having an effective strategy is the key (for some of you) to paying much less than what you borrowed.

Those things that help you plan your strategy are what I will discuss in the remainder of this book. So in the words of Young Jeezy, "Let's get it."

==================

PART I
FEDERAL STUDENT LOANS

==================

CHAPTER 1
TYPES OF FEDERAL STUDENT LOANS

There are two federal student loan programs: Direct Loans and Perkins Loans. A few years ago, there was another federal student loan program: the Federal Family Educational Loan program. For one reason or another, Congress scrapped that program. Loans remain outstanding from that program (and other minor programs), however. And because they remain outstanding, those loans remain an issue for borrowers.

Here's a brief breakdown of the Direct Loan, Perkins Loan, and FFEL Loan programs.

Direct Loans

Congress created the Direct Loan program as part of the Student Loan Reform Act of 1993. Under this program, the federal government directly issues loans to the student. The Direct Loan program was designed to cut the middlemen — private lenders and guaranty agencies — from the loan origination process.

The decision to cut middlemen from the loan process made so much sense that almost two decades later Congress eliminated Federal Family Education Loans. By doing that, Congress made Direct Loans the main source of federal student loans for borrowers.

◆ Read more about how the government came to be your student lender at: http://www.huffingtonpost.com/2013/07/19/history-of-student-loans_n_3622709.html.

The Direct Loan Program offers three types of federal student loans:

○ Stafford loans (which can be subsidized or unsubsidized);
○ PLUS Loans (originally named Parent Loans for Undergraduate Students); and
○ Consolidation Loans.

Direct Stafford Loans (Subsidized and unsubsidized)

The government offers subsidized Stafford Loans to undergraduate students who've demonstrated financial need. The loan is subsidized because the borrower doesn't pay interest before repayment begins or during any deferment.

Unsubsidized student loans are awarded to any qualifying borrower, regardless of financial need. The loan is unsubsidized because the borrower is responsible for interest charged during all periods — even when the borrower is in school, in a grace period, or in a deferment.

Direct PLUS Loan

A Parent PLUS Loan allows a parent to borrow a loan to help pay for the education of her child attending an undergraduate school. Unlike other federal student loans, the borrower has to be credit worthy to get the loan.

◆ Get tips on what to do if you were denied a Parent PLUS Loan because of your credit at: https://www.edvisors.com/college-loans/terms/adverse-credit-history/.

A Graduate PLUS Loan allows you to borrow enough money in federal student loans to cover the full cost of graduate school, including reasonable living costs, if you're a graduate or professional degree student. Like Parent PLUS Loans, you must be credit worthy to get the loan. If rejected, you may still get the Graduate PLUS Loan. But you'll have to find a credit worthy cosigner.

Credit worthiness for Parent & Graduate PLUS Loans is measured by federal regulations rather than your FICO score. Those regulations say that you must not have an adverse credit history to be eligible for a PLUS Loan. You have an adverse credit history if you're at least 90 days delinquent on any debt or if you have a derogatory event on your report in the past five years. A derogatory event can be a:

- default status;
- bankruptcy discharge;
- foreclosure;
- repossession;
- tax lien;
- wage garnishment; or a
- write-off of a Title IV debt.

Even if you have an adverse credit history and can't get a cosigner, you still may get a PLUS Loan. To get the loan, you'll have to prove to your lender that extenuating circumstances exist.

Direct Consolidation loan

A Direct Consolidation Loan lets you combine your federal student loans into one loan. The benefits of consolidation include:

- Escaping default quickly;
- Having to make just one monthly payment to one servicer;
- Reducing your monthly payment by extending your payment term (borrowers usually enroll in income-based-repayment, which has a 25 year repayment term); and
- Lowering your interest rate (borrowers with older loans benefit the most because those loans typically have higher interest rates or variable interest rates, or both.)

Visit studentloans.gov to apply for consolidation.

◆ Learn more about consolidating your loans at http://www.nerdwallet.com/blog/nerdscholar/2013/consolidate-student-loans/.

Joint Consolidation Loan

Before 1 July 2006, the Department of Education offered one other type of consolidation loan: the joint consolidation loan. This loan was for married borrowers who agreed to combine their federal student loan debt and to each be held responsible for the new loan. And even if they later divorced, they each remained liable for the entire loan. As Kanye told Jay, "That shit cray."

◆ Joint consolidation loans have special rules when it comes to payment plans, forgiveness, and cancellation. I highlight those difference in the appropriate sections of this book.

Perkins Loan

Unlike Direct Loans, Perkins Loans are originated and serviced by schools — not the government. (Perkins Loans are backed by the federal government.) Because the school is the lender, all payments and requests for a lower payment amount, deferment, forbearance, forgiveness, and cancellation must be made to the school.

Federal Family Education Loan

Congress created the FFEL program as part of the Higher Education Act of 1965. Under the program, private lenders — as opposed to the federal government — loaned money to students. The federal government guaranteed those loans. So if a borrower ever failed to repay his FFEL loan the government would buy the loan to try and collect it.

There used to be four different types of FFEL Loans:

- Subsidized Federal Stafford Loans;
- Unsubsidized Federal Stafford Loans;
- FFEL PLUS loans; and
- FFEL Consolidation Loans.

FFEL loans stopped being issued in 2010. Now all federal student loans are issued under the Direct Loan Program.

◆ Curious about the FFEL program's creation? Read more at: http://www.dailyfinance.com/2010/03/30/how-the-banks-student-loan-gravy-train-finally-got-halted/.

CHAPTER 2

It's crazy how many of my clients had no clue who they owed their student loans. They didn't know if their loans were federal or private or if their loans were with Navient or FedLoan Servicing. They just knew that they owed a lot of money.

Because they didn't know who they owed, before we could develop their repayment strategy we had to get that information. The easiest way to do that is to access the National Student Loan Data System. That System has information on all your federal student loans.

You access the system by using your personal identification number. That PIN is the same one you used to e-sign your FAFSA paperwork. (If you can't remember that PIN, visit pin.ed.gov.)

Once you're in the System, you'll be able to tell:

- When you first borrowed the loan;
- Whose your current servicer;
- Whose your current lender;
- Whose your current guaranty agency; (You'll have a guaranty agency if you have a Federal Family Education Loan;)
- How much you owe in principal and interest;
- What's your interest rate and whether that rate is fixed or variable; and
- The status of your payment. (Are you current, late, or in default? Or are you in deferment or forbearance?)

You might notice that one company, say Great Lakes Higher Education, has more than one role with your student loan. There's nothing inherently wrong with that company handling multiple roles. It just might make it confusing for you to keep track of who is doing what with your loans.

Once you have your federal student loan information, store it all in one place. I store mine on a Google Docs spreadsheet. A few of my clients are more old school than Blue (You're my boy Blue!) and prefer to use pen and paper. Whether you prefer Sheets or pen a paper, choose a tool, use the tool, and track your loans. It makes repayment much easier.

CHAPTER 3

Talk all the noise you want about your federal student loans but they're much better than your private student loans. Unlike your favorite Sallie, the government makes it easy — some say, too damn easy — to pay them back for financing your education.

You have four major repayment options to choose from:

o   Standard Repayment;
o   Pay As You Earn;
o   Income-Based-Repayment; and
o   Income-Contingent-Repayment.

When your six month grace period ends, you're automatically enrolled in the Standard Repayment plan. If you want to be enrolled in one of the income-driven-repayment plans — that is, the PAYE, IBR, and ICR plans — submit the IDR plan application designating which of the three you want to be enrolled in to each of your student loan servicers. Depending on your servicer, you can submit your IDR application online, by mail, or by fax.

◆   To get an estimate of your monthly payment under each of the plans, use the Department of Education's repayment estimator at: https://studentloans.gov/myDirectLoan/mobile/repayment/repaymentEstimator.action.

Let's break down the four plans so you understand how each works.

Standard Repayment

The Standard Repayment plan, which is available for all your federal student loans, is the cheapest and fastest way to repay your federal student loans. It's the cheapest because you'll pay less in interest compared to the IDR plans. And it's the fastest because you'll finish repaying your loans within 10 years. (The IDR plans all take at least 20 years to complete.)

Those are the benefits of the Standard plan.

There's a major drawback though: your monthly payment will be higher under the Standard plan than it would under any other.

Pay As You Earn

In 2011, President Obama caused the PAYE plan to be launched. The PAYE plan, which lasts for 2o years, promises to help student loan borrowers deal with their debt by capping borrowers' monthly payments at 10% of their discretionary income. And no matter what a borrower's income is, the amount she would pay under the PAYE plan will never be greater than what her payment would be under the Standard Repayment plan.

That capped monthly payment amount is just one of the PAYE plan's benefits. Other benefits include:

- not capitalizing your interest if you have a partial financial hardship and capping your capitalized interest at 10% if you have no partial financial hardship;
- granting you a partial interest subsidy for your first three years of repayment;

- allowing your payments to be eligible for the Public Service Loan Forgiveness program; and
- forgiving any remaining balance after you've made 20 years of payments.

There are at least three drawbacks to the PAYE plan. First, you'll pay more interest than you would under the Standard Plan. That's because you'll be repaying the loan for 20 years rather than the Standard Repayment plan's 10 years. Second, you must reapply each year for the PAYE plan. Third, any balance forgiven after 20 years may be treated as taxable income.

There are four eligibility requirements for the PAYE plan.

1. You must have the right loan;
2. You must have gotten your first loan after 30 September 2007;
3. You must have gotten a loan disbursement after 30 September 2011; and
4. You must have a partial financial hardship.

You have the right loan if your loan isn't in default and is something other than:

- A PLUS Loan made to a parent;
- A Direction Consolidation Loan that includes a Parent PLUS loans; and
- An Unconsolidated FFEL and Federal Perkins Loan.

You meet the second and third requirements if (a) you borrowed a student loan for the first time during the 2008–09 school year and (b) you were still in school during the 2011–12 school year.

And you have a partial financial hardship if your annual loan repayment under the Standard plan is greater than the annual repayment you'd make under the PAYE plan. Typically, higher income borrowers have difficulty meeting this hardship standard unless they have high student loan balances.

◆ Use the income driven repayment application to apply for the PAYE plan. Send the application and proof of your income (typically your tax return) to each student loan servicer that has loans you can pay under the PAYE plan.

◆ On 9 June 2014, the President issued a memorandum directing the Department of Education expand the PAYE plan to additional Direct Loan borrowers. The memorandum isn't clear which additional borrowers will be affected. Whatever changes there will be are expected to occur before the end of 2015.

Income-Based-Repayment

In 2009, the government began offering the IBR plan. When originally launched, that plan capped all borrower's payments under the plan at 15% of their discretionary income and forgave the balance that remained after a borrower made 25 years of payments. That plan was later strengthened by capping new borrowers' payments at 10% and cutting their time for forgiveness from 25 years to 20 years of payments. (You're a new borrower if you got your first loan disbursement as of 1 July 2014.)

Besides capping the payment amount and forgiving the balance at 20 or 25 years, the IBR plan also benefits you by limiting the capitalization of your interest for the first three years of repayment.

The drawbacks of the IBR plan are the same as they are for the PAYE plan: you'll pay more in interest; you'll have to apply each year; and you'll likely pay taxes on the amount forgiven.

You're eligible for the IBR plan if you have (a) a partial financial hardship and (b) a Direct Loan or FFEL Loan. Two follow up points to those requirements. First, as is true with the PAYE plan, you have a partial financial hardship if your payment under the Standard plan would be greater than your payment under the IBR plan. Second, a loan that's in default and a Direct Consolidation Loan that repaid a Parent PLUS Loan aren't eligible for repayment under the IBR plan.

Borrowers who attended graduate school benefit the most under the IBR plan. That's because a graduate student can rack up a high federal student loan balance and then repay his student loans under the IBR plan and make low payments for several years and have his balance forgiven.

◆ The IBR plan has been criticized for its economic implications. Seemingly in response to that criticism, the Department of Education's fiscal year 2015 budget proposal suggested reform to student loan repayment, including the IBR plan. (The student loan reform proposal starts at page S-13 of the proposal.) Despite the Department's proposed reform efforts, some still argue more needs to be done.

◆ What does all that mean for you if you're already in repayment? I'm not sure. Student loan gurus Bill Penn and Heather Jarvis believe those already in repayment and those in school will continue to use existing repayment plans under the same or similar terms.

Income-Contingent-Repayment

Of the income-driven-repayment plans, the ICR plan is the oldest. Launched in the early 90's, the ICR plan, which requires repayment for 25 years, was designed to benefit low income borrowers and borrowers wanting to pursue public service careers. Under the ICR plan, monthly payments are capped at 20% of your discretionary income.

The benefits of the ICR plan are that:

o   You don't have to have a partial financial hardship to qualify for the plan;
o   Your capitalized interest is capped at 10% of the loan amount;
o   Your remaining loan balance is forgiven after you've made 25 years of payments; and
o   Unlike the PAYE and IBR plans, your Direct Consolidation Loan that repaid a Parent PLUS Loan or a Perkins Loan (or both), and your Graduate PLUS Loan qualify for repayment under the ICR plan.

The drawbacks of the ICR plan are the same as they are for the PAYE and the IBR plan: you'll pay more in interest; you'll have to apply each year; and you'll likely pay taxes on the amount that's forgiven. And in addition to those three, there's a fourth: there's no interest subsidy for the first three years of repayment under the plan.

Repayment plan extras

Calculating payment under PAYE and IBR. Under the PAYE and IBR plans your payment is calculated by taking 15% (or by 10% for PAYE and some IBR plan borrowers) of your discretionary income. To find your discretionary income, subtract 150% of the poverty guideline for your family size and location from your adjusted gross income. The remaining amount is your annual discretionary income. Once you have that amount, multiply it by 15% (or if you're a new borrower, 10%) and then divide that amount by 12. That final number is your monthly payment amount under the PAYE plan or the IBR plan.

Calculating payment under ICR. Under the ICR plan, your payment is the lesser of 20% of (a) your discretionary income (use the same formula as you would for the PAYE or IBR plans) or (b) what you would pay on a repayment plan with a fixed payment over 12 years, adjusted to your income. Instead of doing the math yourself, use the Repayment Estimator at studentloans.gov.

Proof of income under IDR plans. Provide a copy of your tax return from this year or last as proof of your income. You may need to provide alternative proof if you haven't filed a tax return in the past two years or if last year's AGI differs significantly from what you're earning now. If you have to provide alternative proof, provide a pay stub or other proof of your income such as (1) a letter from your employer listing your income; (2) a copy of your interest or bank statement; (3) a copy of your dividend statements; or (4) a letter from you explaining the source of your income and giving the name and address of the source. And if you have no income, indicate that on your application.

You can have a zero dollar payment. Under the income driven repayment plans, your monthly payment may be zero. A zero dollar payment counts towards forgiveness under the repayment plans and under the Public Service Loan Forgiveness program.

You can have nonconsecutive payments. To qualify for term forgiveness (that is, forgiveness at 20 or 25 years) under the income-driven-repayment plans, your payments don't have to be consecutive. You just have to make 20 or 25 years of payment. So if you take 30 years to make 25 years of payment, so be it.

Tax issues after forgiveness. After you've made 20 or 25 years of payments under the particular income driven repayment plan and you're eligible for forgiveness, the IRS will treat the forgiven amount as taxable income. You may have that forgiven amount excluded from your taxable income depending on your situation. Speak with a tax professional to learn more about this exclusion

You have to recertify annually. Under the income-driven-repayment plans you have to recertify your income and family size annually. This should happen within 35 days of the date you certified the year before. You're supposed to get a reminder to recertify within 60–90 days of your anniversary date. If you don't recertify your income, your monthly payment will jump to what it would be under the Standard plan. And if you don't certify your family size, your family size will be one for that year.

Mid-year changes in your income. If you lost your job or if your salary decreased after you certified your income, submit proof of your job or salary loss so your payment can be recalculated.

Proof of income. Since income-driven-repayment plans are based on your income, you have to provide proof of what your income is. Most borrowers provide a copy of their previous year's tax return, which shows their adjusted gross income for that year. If your AGI doesn't reflect what you're currently making, you must submit additional proof of your income. Typically, this can be a recent pay stub or a letter from your employer stating how much you earn and how often you're paid.

Joint consolidation loans. If you and your current (or former spouse) have a joint consolidation loan, you may repay under the IBR plan if both of you have a partial financial hardship.

Married couples payment. Your spouse's income will be considered under the income-driven-repayment plans if you file taxes jointly. But if you file separately, only your AGI will be considered. And if you want, you and your spouse may repay your student loan bills together. I don't know why you and bae would do that. (Side note: I hate the term "bae" for these four reasons: http://wapo.st/1NYWMmz.) But you might. So just know that you can make your payment together. If you ever want to stop paying together, resubmit an income-driven-repayment application requesting that separation.

Same-sex married couples. If your spouse is the same sex as you, you're considered married for income-driven-repayment purposes if you got married in a jurisdiction that recognizes same sex marriages. And that remains true even if you no longer live in that jurisdiction. The Department of Education calls this the "place of celebration" rule.

No longer have a partial financial hardship. You may stay in your PAYE or IBR plan even if you no longer have a partial financial hardship or no longer want to make payments based on your income. When that happens, your payments won't exceed what you would've paid under the Standard plan when you first entered the PAYE or IBR plan.

Switching plans. If you're in the PAYE, IBR, or ICR plans, you may change your repayment plan to any other repayment plan. Except if you're in the IBR plan, you must first make one payment under the Standard plan before switching to another repayment plan.

At some point you will need (or want) a break from repaying your student loans. Maybe you're trying to take that life changing trip to the Far East, or maybe, like some of my friends, you're trying to get to Vegas for the Pacquiao-Mayweather fight or whatever's the hot ticket at the time you're reading this. Or maybe you have a legitimate reason such as unemployment or caring for an ill family member. (Who am I kidding, going YOLO is always a legitimate reason. Right?)

No matter your reason, if you want to take a timeout from repaying your federal student loans without worrying about default, request either a deferment or a forbearance.

Deferment

A deferment under the federal student loan program allows you to stop paying your loans for a period. This is a good strategy to use if you're unemployed or if you're:

o   Attending school at least half-time;
o   Participating in a graduate fellowship;
o   Attending a rehabilitation training program;
o   Suffering an economic hardship; or
o   Serving in the military.

Because getting deferments for attending school, participating in a graduate fellowship, and serving in the military are rather straightforward, let's focus on the deferments for an economic hardship and unemployment.

◆ If you have Direct Loans or FFEL Loans issued to you before 1 July 1993 or if you have Perkins Loans, you may be eligible for other deferments. Speak to your loan servicer to find out more about your additional deferment options.

Economic hardship

The economic hardship deferment is granted one year at a time for a maximum of three years. And it applies to your Direct Loans, FFEL Loans, and Perkins Loans. There are four ways to qualify for the economic hardship deferment, the first three are automatically granted if you provide support. The three "automatic" deferments occur when:

○ You qualified previously for an economic hardship deferment under another federal loan program;
○ You're receiving federal or state public assistance benefits such as SSI or food stamps; or
○ You're serving as a Peace Corps volunteer.

The fourth way to qualify for the economic hardship deferment requires a little math. You qualify if you're working full time and your monthly income doesn't exceed the larger of:

○ The federal minimum wage rate; or
○ 150% of the poverty line income for your family size and state. (In 2014, the poverty line for a family of two living in the 48 contiguous states is $15,730. And a 150% of that is $23,595.)

You're working full time if you're expected to work for at least three consecutive months at 30 hours per week. You can calculate your monthly income by taking (a) the income from your employment and other sources before taxes and other deductions; or (b) one-twelfth of the amount you reported as "adjusted gross income" on your most recently filed federal income tax return. And your family size includes you, your spouse, your children, your unborn child that will be born during the deferment period, and anyone else who gets more than half their support from you. Support includes money, housing, food, clothes, and medical and dental care.

The Student Loan Borrower Assistance has a self-help packet you can use to request an economic hardship deferment. Get the packet at: http://bit.ly/1PrM2R7.

Unemployment hardship

You can qualify for an unemployment deferment for your Direct, FFEL, and Perkins Loans in one of two ways. The first way is the easiest: just provide proof that you're eligible to receive unemployment benefits. The second way to qualify is to show that within six months before applying for the deferment you made six diligent attempts to get full time employment. Typically, you prove your diligence by (a) certifying that you're seeking but cannot find full-time employment and (b) showing that you've registered with a public or private employment agency.

The unemployment deferment typically lasts for six months. You can reapply for another six month deferment at the end of the preceding period.

◆ You can qualify for the unemployment deferment even if you've never been an employee before.

Benefits & drawbacks of deferment

Aside from stopping repayment of your student loans, there are at least two benefits of placing your loans in deferment. First, interest doesn't accrue on subsidized loans during the deferment. The same isn't true of your unsubsidized loans. Those continue accruing interest. You can, however, pay just the accruing interest on your deferred unsubsidized loans. Do this if you can. You'll avoid having to pay interest on your interest (that's roughly what capitalization causes you to do) when your deferment ends. Second, if the loan is deferred, it isn't in default, and you won't be subject to collection attempts or lawsuits. Plus, you'll remain eligible for additional education assistance.

Except for pushing your repayment further into the future, I can't think of any real drawbacks of deferment. But that's not really a drawback. That's exactly what you want.

Applying for deferment

To apply for the non-automatic deferments, submit a request to your loan servicer. And if you have more than one servicer, send a request to each one.

Eligibility

If you have Direct Loans, FFEL Loans, or Perkins Loans, or a combination of all three, and those loans aren't in default, you're generally eligible for deferment. You still must meet the requirements for the deferment you're requesting.

- Your defaulted loans regain their eligibility for deferment when you get out of default. The two ways to get out of default are to consolidate or rehabilitate your student loans.

Deferment extras

Parent PLUS Loans. Deferments under Parent PLUS loans are based on the parent borrower's eligibility — not the student's. So if you're a Parent PLUS Loan borrower, you may defer repaying the PLUS loan if you're unemployed or if you're (1) attending school at least halftime; (2) studying in an approved graduate fellowship or rehabilitation program for the disabled; or (3) experiencing economic hardship (up to three years). You also defer repayment of the PLUS Loan while your child is attending school at least half time.

Resetting deferment time limit. If you combine your federal student loans into a Direct Consolidation Loan, your time limits for deferment resets. And that makes senses right? The Direct Consolidation Loan is, a new loan.

Forbearance

Putting your loans in forbearance accomplishes mostly the same things a deferment does. The major difference is that forbearance isn't as helpful as deferment because interest continues accruing on all loans, subsidized or unsubsidized. Despite that difference, forbearance does what it's supposed to: temporarily stop repayment of your loan.

There are three categories of forbearances:

- Poor health;
- Administrative; and
- Mandatory.

Poor Health. You can get a forbearance if you're in poor health or have other personal problems affecting your ability to make the scheduled payments. A forbearance for poor health is granted for up to a year at a time. There are no limits to the number of years that can be granted.

Administrative. You can get an administrative forbearance for many reasons, including:

- A deferment was granted but your lender later learns that you didn't qualify for the deferment;
- A period during which payments were overdue before your deferment began;
- A period necessary to determine your eligibility for bankruptcy discharge, closed school discharge, or similar discharges; or
- A period of delinquency that may remain after deferment or mandatory forbearance and before the next due date is established.

Mandatory

You can get a mandatory forbearance if:

- You're serving in a medical or dental internship or residency program and you're not eligible for the internship deferment formerly available in the FFEL program;

- You're serving in a national service position for which you received a national service education award under Americorps (the National and Community Service Trust Act of 1993); or
- You're eligible for partial repayment of a loan under one of federal student loan repayment programs.

Benefits & drawbacks of forbearance

The major benefit of forbearance is its ability to prevent you from defaulting on your student loans by temporarily stopping or reducing your monthly payment. And you want to avoid defaulting on your student loans so you don't have to worry about being sued or having your tax refund or Social Security benefits being taken, or wages garnished. Another benefit appears when you're attempting to finance a major purchase such as a home. Forbearance (and deferment) benefits you by temporarily reducing your monthly debt to income ratio, which might allow you to qualify for better loan terms or to get approved for a greater amount.

The drawback is that interest continues to accrue on your loans. But if you got more month than money, does it matter if interest continues accruing?

Applying for forbearance

You typically won't have to complete an application to place your loans in forbearance. Call your loan servicer and explain to them your reason for requesting forbearance and they'll grant it over the phone. When an application is required, consider using the general forbearance request form for Direct Loans, the Teacher

Loan Forgiveness form, or the Mandatory Forbearance request form provided by the Department of Education.

Forbearance extras

FFEL Loan and Direct Loan regulations are similar. The regulations controlling forbearances for Direct Loans and FFEL are similar but not the same. The FFEL regulations distinguish between discretionary and mandatory forbearances. The Direct Loan regulations don't.

Low income FFEL Loan borrowers. If you have a low income and cannot repay your FFEL loan within the maximum repayment term — typically 10 years — you can get a mandatory administrative forbearance for up to five years.

Teachers with FFEL Loans. If you're a teacher, you can get a mandatory forbearance while you're performing teaching service that would qualify you for teacher loan forgiveness.

Perkins Loan forbearance. As a Perkins Loan borrower, you can place that loan in forbearance if (a) your total federal student loan payment is at least 20% of your total monthly income; (b) you're in poor health or you have other "acceptable reasons"; or (c) you're affected by a national military mobilization or other national emergency. There's typically a three year cap on the length of a Perkins loan forbearance.

Applying for a Direct Consolidation Loan or forgiveness. If you're considering applying for a consolidation loan or loan forgiveness or cancellation, request an administrative forbearance so you're not paying on a loan that may no longer exist.

Joint consolidation loans + PLUS loans with a cosigner. Your lender will grant a forbearance only if you and your joint borrower can't make the scheduled payments.

CHAPTER 5

Before getting into if you should consolidate your federal student loans, let's start at the beginning: what is federal student loan consolidation? Simply put, federal student loan consolidation is where you take multiple loans (almost any federal student loan will dO) and turn them into one new Direct Consolidation Loan.

An alternative to consolidating your federal student loans into a Direct Consolidation Loan is to refinance your federal student loans into a new private loan. If you refinance with a private lender, you typically can combine your federal student loans with your private student loans.

Whether you should consolidate your student loans using the federal program or whether you should refinance using a private lender depends on you. Depends on your goals, your income, your credit score, and so on and so on.

Instead of answering that subjective question within these pages, allow me to direct you to writings from The Huffington Post, the Consumer Financial Protection Bureau, and Time. These writings may help your decide if refinancing your federal student loans with a private lender is right for you.

For now, let's focus on better understanding federal student loan consolidation. Let's start with the benefits and drawbacks.

Benefits and drawbacks of consolidation

The benefits of consolidating include:

- Getting out of default faster than if you rehabilitated your defaulted student loans (consolidation happens in about 90 days; rehabilitation takes you about 270 days);
- Having a smaller monthly payment (you have up to 30 years to repay a Direct Consolidation Loan);
- Having only one lender and only one monthly payment; and
- Refreshing previously exhausted deferment options.

There are at least three drawbacks of consolidation. First, the interest rates on some of your loans may increase. When you consolidate, your new interest rate is the weighted average of the interest rates of all the loans you're consolidating. So if you have loans with an interest rate of 4% and others with 8%, your new consolidation loan will have an interest rate somewhere in between those two percentages.

Second, if you consolidate a Perkins Loan, you'll lose your cancellation rights under that program. That's because after you consolidate a Perkins Loan with your other loans, the resulting loan has its own forgiveness and cancellation provisions.

Finally, if you consolidate your Parent PLUS Loan with your other federal student loans, the resulting Direct Consolidation Loan won't be eligible for repayment under the income-based-repayment plan. Stated differently, having a Parent PLUS Loan as part of a consolidation loan means you can't repay that loan using the IBR plan.

Eligibility

You're eligible for a Direct Consolidation Loan if you have at least one outstanding Direct Loan or FFEL Loan. If you're in default on a federal student loan, you can get out of default by consolidating that loan with other federal student loans. But if the loan you've defaulted on has a garnishment order associated with it or it has been reduced to a judgment, you can't consolidate that loan until the garnishment order is lifted or the judgment is removed.

If you're consolidating a loan that's in default, you may be charged collection costs of up to 18.5% of the outstanding principal and interest of the defaulted loan.

Applying for a Direct Consolidation Loan

You can apply for a Direct Consolidation Loan using a paper application or the website at studentloans.gov. I advise my clients to use the online process because it's simple to use. Plus, it allows you to input your income so you can project what your monthly payment would be on the resulting Direct Consolidation Loan.

After you submit the application

The consolidation process takes about three months to complete. Until that day comes, you're still responsible for making payments on your loans. If you want to avoid repaying your loans until your loans are consolidated, request a deferment or forbearance from your loan's servicer. Do this for each loan you're consolidating.

Consolidation extras

Be prepared to resubmit your income-driven-repayment application. In my experience, I've routinely had to resubmit my clients' applications for income-driven-repayment. I don't know how the application get's lost — I always fax and mail the application — but it does. So be prepared to resubmit yours.

No payments required when consolidating a defaulted loan. If you're in default on a federal student loan, you can get a Direct Consolidation Loan by agreeing to repay the consolidation loan through an income-driven-repayment plan.

Consolidate a defaulted Direct Consolidation Loan. If you're in default on your Direct Consolidation Loan, you can reconsolidate it if you have another eligible loan that's not in default. For example, if you're in default on your Direct Consolidation Loan and you have a FFEL Loan, you may consolidate those two loans together into a new Direct Consolidation Loan.

Reconsolidating a FFEL Loan. You may reconsolidate a FFEL Loan that's in default if you want to consolidate that loan into a Direct Consolidation Loan so you can enroll in the income based or income contingent repayment plans.

Consolidating a joint consolidation loan. Neither you nor the spouse you jointly consolidated your loans with may reconsolidate that joint consolidation loan. As of now, you're stuck with that loan until it's paid off or you die.

A bunch of programs will help you get rid of your loans. Recently, SALT — an American Student Assistance creation — cobbled together an almost exhaustive list of over 60 ways to get rid of your student loans.

Of that list, let's talk about three: Public Service Loan Forgiveness, Teacher Loan Forgiveness, and Perkins Loan Cancelation.

Public Service Loan Forgiveness

This program is the best of the bunch. It forgives your remaining Direct Loans after you've made 120 monthly payments. You'll get the greatest benefit of this program if you have a low paying job, you have a high federal student loan balance, and you're repaying through an income-driven-repayment plan.

To qualify for forgiveness, do four things.

1. **Work the right job**. You must work a full time paying job (usually over 30 hours) for the government, 501(c)(3), and other select employers.

♦ The Consumer Finance Protection Bureau reports that about 25% of people in the United States have a job that qualifies for the Public Service Loan Forgiveness Program. So don't assume your job doesn't qualify.

2. **Make the right payments**. You should be enrolled in an income-driven-repayment plan (most borrowers who work for a qualifying employer enroll in IBR) and make your payments within 20 days of the date they're due.
3. **Make the payments 120 times**. You must make 120 monthly payments. The payments don't have to be in a row. So say you take a five year break from working the right job, when you return to the right job you'll pick back up with the number of payments you've already made that counted towards forgiveness.
4. **Certify annually**. Although not mandatory, certify your employment annually using the form provided by the Department of Education.

Four notes on PSLF. First, if you have a Parent PLUS loan you're eligible based on your own job. You probably should consolidate that loan to take full advantage of the forgiveness program. That's because your Parent PLUS Loan doesn't qualify for an income-driven-repayment plan. But if you consolidate that PLUS loan, the resulting loan becomes eligible for the ICR plan.

Second, if you have a FFEL Loan, consolidate it into a Direct Consolidation Loan to take advantage of PSLF. Only loans made under the Direct Loan program are eligible for Public Service Loan Forgiveness.

Third, if you have a joint consolidation loan, you're eligible for forgiveness. But to forgive the whole loan under the program both you and the spouse you consolidated the loan with have to meet the program's requirements. So if you meet the requirements but your spouse doesn't, your loan balance will be forgiven but you're still jointly responsible for your spouse's portion of the loan.

Finally, you can qualify for the program even if you work for an organization engaged in religious activities, such as a church. Your full time duties, however, must be unrelated to religious instructions or any proselytizing.

◆ Check out the Department of Education's information sheet on the Public Service Loan Forgiveness for more answers.

Certifying public service work

Although not required, complete an employment certification form for the PSLF program. That form confirms you worked full time for a qualifying employer during the previous year. You and an authorized official from your employer must complete the form. I advise my clients to complete it during their open benefits enrollment period or at the beginning of their company's fiscal year.

Make sure you keep a copy of that form. You'll likely have to resubmit it when the time comes to have your federal student loans forgiven.

Teacher Loan Forgiveness

This program is for you if you have Stafford or Direct Loans and you teach full time for five consecutive years in a designated elementary or secondary school or educational service agency serving low income families.

The amount that can be forgiven varies but isn't more than $17,500 total. You get the most forgiven if you're a highly qualified full time math or science teacher in an eligible secondary school. You can also get the highest amount if you're a highly qualified special education teacher and meet other requirements.

You're highly qualified if the state's certified you as a teacher or if you've passed the state's teacher licensing exam. With limited exceptions, you must also hold a state license.

◆ Visit tateesq.com for more information on Teacher Loan Forgiveness.

Perkins Loan Cancelation

This program is for you if you have a Perkins Loan and you teach full time for at least one year. You must either:

○ Teach at a low income school;
○ Teach special education;
○ Teach math, science, foreign languages, or bilingual education; or
○ Teach in a field that has a shortage of qualified teachers in your state.

After your first year of teaching, 15% of your outstanding Perkins Loans will be canceled. The second year, another percentage will be canceled. The third year, another. Then another in the fourth year. And then at the end of the fifth year, your entire Perkins Loan debt will be canceled.

To apply for Perkins Loan cancellation, contact the school you got the loan from and ask about the cancellation process.

Tax issues and student loan forgiveness

A few years ago, the Treasury Department issued a letter stating that Teacher Loan Forgiveness and Public Service Loan Forgiveness meet the requirements for income exclusion under the Internal Revenue Code. Those types of forgiveness programs meet the exclusion requirements because forgiveness is tied to you working for a period in a qualifying public service position.

Forgiveness under the income-driven-repayment plans, however, is treated as taxable income.

CHAPTER 7
CANCELLING YOUR LOANS

The great thing about federal student loans is they have built in cancellation provisions. So if you're a parent and you took out a Parent PLUS Loan to help pay for your child's education, don't worry about the Department of Education calling you for repayment after your daughter dies or has been murdered. (That's what happened to the parents of Lauren Tanski. A short time after their daughter was murdered, Sallie Mae called looking to collect on the roughly $60 thousand Lauren owed in private student loans at her death. Read the Tanski's story here: http://bit.ly/1OiixQa.)

For some of you, my inclusion of Lauren's story may be seen as low key (high key?) macabre or even distasteful. I get that. But I also get that collection attempts from family members after a borrower's death happen every day. And what better example than Lauren's of the lengths a private lender will go to collect?

Unlike private student loans, there are several reasons your student loans can be cancelled, including:

o You become totally and permanently disabled;
o You die (or if it's a Parent PLUS Loan, your parent(s) die);
o Your school closed while you were still enrolled;
o Your school falsely certified (using forgery or identity theft) your eligibility for federal student loans; and
o Your school failed to pay a refund it owed you.

Of these discharges, the loan discharge for your total and permanent disability is the one I see the most often.

Consequently, I'm going to go more in depth with that discharge than I will with the others.

Having said that, I recognize that some of you may want more information about the other discharges than what I provided here. To help get you that information, I've included links to my website and other sites that go into depth greater than I do here. And if that's not enough for you, email me at tate@tateesq.com and I'll try and get you the information you need.

Total and permanent disability discharge

You're eligible for a total and permanent disability discharge if your doctor certifies that you can't engage in any substantial gainful activity by reason of a medically determinable physical or mental impairment that:

- Can be expected to result in death;
- Has lasted for a continuous period of not less than 60 months; or
- Can be expected to last for a continuous period of not less than 60 months.

What does substantial gainful activity mean

Substantial gainful activity means a level of work performed for pay or profit that involves significant physical or mental activities or a combination of both. Worked performed for profit covers people who are self-employed.

Substantial gainful activity doesn't refer to income from sources other than employment. The Department won't consider non-employment income when determining if you're capable of substantial gainful activity.

Other ways to show you're totally and permanently disabled

You can also show you're totally and permanently disabled if:

- You're a veteran of the armed forces and you submit documentation from the U.S. Department of Veterans Affairs showing that the VA has determined that you are unemployable due to a service-connected disability; or
- You're getting Social Security Disability Insurance or Supplemental Security Income benefits and you submit a Social Security Administration notice of award for SSDI or SSI benefits stating your next scheduled disability review will be within 5 to 7 years from your most recent SSA disability determination.

Documents to provide when requesting a TPD discharged based on your doctor's certification

Don't provide any other documents when you're requesting a TPD discharge based on your doctor's certification. Your doctor's signature is sufficient.

When you're completing sections 1 thru 3 of the TPD discharge application have your doctor — who must be a licensed doctor of medicine or osteopathy — complete section 4. After that, apply to Nelnet within 90 days of your doctor completing her section. (The Department of Education hired Nelnet to process all TPD applications.)

Veteran certification

If you're a veteran, you can skip having a doctor sign the TPD discharge application and instead submit documentation from the VA showing that the VA has determined:

- You have a service connected disability (or disabilities) that is 100% disabling; or
- You're totally disabled based on an individual employability determination.

SSDI or SSI benefit certification

If you're getting either SSDI or SSI benefits, you too can skip having a doctor sign the TPD discharge application and instead submit a Social Security Administration notice of award for SSDI or SSI benefits. That notice must state your next scheduled disability review will be within five to seven years from your most recent SSA disability determination.

Loans eligible for TPD discharge

Your FFELs, Direct Loans, and Perkins Loans are eligible for disability discharge. And if you're a parent who took out a Parent PLUS Loan, you can discharge that loan if you're suffering a total and permanent disability. If your spouse cosigned on that loan with you, she will still be responsible for the loan.

Loans disbursed under the Health Education Assistance Loan program are also eligible for TPD discharge. The Secretary of Health and Human Services may discharge your HEAL loan if it finds you have a total and permanent disability. To apply, provide the Secretary with medical evidence substantiating your disability claim. That evidence must be less than four months old.

Under the HEAL program, total and permanent disability is defined differently. You must be "unable to engage in any substantial gainful activity because of a medically determinable impairment, which the Secretary [of Health and Human Services] expects to continue for a long and indefinite period of time or to result in death."

Joint consolidation loans

You can discharge your portion of the joint consolidation loan if you're totally and permanently disabled. But even though you discharged your portion of the loan, you'll still be jointly responsible for your spouse's portion.

Applying for a TPD discharge

You apply for a total and permanent discharge of your federal student loans by applying online at Nelnet.com or by contacting Nelnet at 888.303.7818, disabilityinformation@nelnet.net, or at U.S. Department of Education, P.O. Box 87130, Lincoln, NE 68501-7130.

After you apply

After you apply, Nelnet will review your application to ensure that it's complete and that you qualify for a discharge. It will also review its records and identify other loans of yours that may qualify for a TPD discharge. After it's done both things, Nelnet will contact your loan holders and instruct them to suspend collection activity on your loans for up to 120 days. During that period you won't have to repay the loans you're trying to discharge.

Once Nelnet confirms your application is accurate and appears to meet the TPD discharge requirements, it will send your application to the Department of Education for a final decision.

Denied application

If the Department denies your application, you have one year from the date you get the denial letter to submit additional information supporting your application. After one year, submit a new TPD discharge application.

Approved application

If the Department approves your application, your eligible federal student loans will be discharged. And they'll remain discharged if over the next three years, your income doesn't exceed the Poverty Guideline amount for a family of two in your state, regardless of your actual family size. In 2015, that amount for everywhere except Hawaii and Alaska is $15,930.

Beware, the Department will reinstate your loans if during the three year monitoring period you:

- Get a new Direct Loan, Perkins Loan, or TEACH grant;
- Fail to return a disbursement of a Direct Loan, Perkins Loan, or TEACH grant you got before your loans were discharged; or
- Get notice from the Social Security Administration that you're no longer totally and permanently disabled.

Multiple loan holders

If your federal student loans are held by more than one holder, you still submit only one TPD discharge application. Nelnet will contact all your holders and will keep them informed throughout the process.

TPD extras

Doctor qualifications. Only doctors of medicine or osteopathy licensed to practice in the United States may certify your application. Medical professionals who can't certify your application include:

- Chiropractors;
- Herbalists;
- Physician assistants;
- Registered nurses;
- Licensed practical nurses,
- Ph.D.s; and
- Residents in training who aren't yet licensed M.D.s or D.O.s.

Taxable income. The IRS considers the discharged debt as taxable income. You may avoid paying taxes on that amount if you're insolvent when you file taxes. Contact a tax professional to determine how a TPD discharge may affect your taxes.

Death discharge

Your death results in your federal student loans being discharged.

Simple.

PLUS Loans are a little trickier. If you have a Parent PLUS Loan, the loan is discharged if your child dies. But if you, the parent, dies, the loan isn't discharged. Your surviving spouse remains liable. You and your spouse must die for that Parent PLUS Loan to be discharged.

To get the discharge, the surviving child or spouse must submit a death certificate or other reliable documentation to the Department of Education.

Closed school discharge

You can get the federal loans you borrowed — Direct Loans, Direct Consolidation Loans, FFEL Loans, and Perkins Loans all qualify if they were borrowed after 1 January 1986 — to attend a certain school if that school closed while you were in attendance.

Closed school discharges occur most frequently at for profit schools. Why is that? Answer: Some for profit schools lose their accreditation or mislead applicants about the quality of education and career placement help they'll get, forcing the school to close its doors. This recently happened at Corinthian owned schools such as Everest Institute, WyoTech, and Heald College.

◆ The Department of Education maintains a database of closed schools. You can search the Departments Closed School Monthly Reports by visiting: www2.ed.gov/offices/OSFAP/PEPS/closed schools.html. That report will give you the schools official closure date.

The closed school discharge has two major limitations. First, the campus that you're attending must be the one that closes. So if you attend school at campus A and campus B closes, you're not eligible for the discharge. But if campus A closes, you would be eligible for the discharge.

Second, if you're attending an online program and your online school closes, you're eligible for the discharge only if the main physical campus closes. And if your online program has no main physical campus, you're out of luck. There is no closed school discharge for a school that's entirely online.

Applying for the closed school discharge

You must apply for this discharge using the school closure application. You'll need the school's closure date to complete the application. When you've completed the application, unless directed otherwise, submit it to your loan servicer.

♦ If you have Direct Loans, FFEL Loans, or Perkins Loans, or a combination of those loans, those loans will be discharged (cancelled) when you die.

False certification discharge

You can discharge your Direct Loans and FFEL Loans if:

- You didn't graduate high school and your school falsely certifies you can benefit from its program;
- Your school falsely certifies you're able to meet minimum state employment requirements for the job that you're being trained for;
- Your school forges your name on the loan papers or check endorsements; and

○ You're a victim of identity theft.

To be honest, if you didn't attend a truck driver or beauty or barber school, or if someone didn't steal your identity like this Pennsylvania couple did, this discharge likely isn't for you. Since few people qualify for this discharge, I won't break it down. Instead, if you want more information on this discharges, you can read more about each on my website or at studentloanborrowerassis-tance.org.

Unpaid refund discharge

You qualify for this discharge if you got Direct Loans and FFEL Loans after 1 January 1986 and your school kept a refund you were entitled to. That means if you enrolled in school but never attended or withdrew from the school and never got a refund you were supposed to get, your loans should be discharged.

The amount discharged is calculated using a formula created by the school or the Department of Education. No matter which formula is used, two pieces of information are needed: the tuition cost and the percentage of the term or course you completed. If that percentage is over 60% of a term or course, you're ineligible for this discharge.

To apply, complete the Department of Education's unpaid refund discharge application.

Discharge extras

School related discharges part 1. A few things happen when you get a school related discharge. First, you'll no longer have to repay the loan. Second, the amount discharged won't be treated as taxable income. Third, any money you paid on that now discharged loan should be refunded. Finally, your credit report should be cleared of any negative information regarding the discharged loan.

School related discharges part 2. You may be eligible for more than one type of discharge. So apply for all the discharges you believe you're eligible for.

Discharges and Direct Consolidation Loans. If you have a Direct Consolidation Loan and you get a school related discharge, only the portion of the loan that's attributable to the school's misconduct will be discharged.

Parent PLUS Loans and school related discharges. You can get your Parent PLUS Loan forgiven if the school your child was attending closed while he attended that school.

School closed within 120 days of withdrawal. If you withdrew from your school within 120 days before the school closed, you still qualify for the closed school discharge. The Department of Education can extend that period for exceptional circumstances or if you attended a correspondence school.

CHAPTER 8

As Ed Lover would say, "C'mon son." You already know how to avoid defaulting on your student loans: pay regularly. And if you can't pay regularly, lower your payment under one of the income driven repayment plans so you can get an amount you can afford or request a deferment or forbearance.

But no matter what you do, don't bury your head in the sand. Be proactive. Because if you're not, you'll learn that the Department of Education has super collection powers that even Dr. Manhattan couldn't mess with.

Let's be clear on when your loans will reach default status. You're in default on your Direct Loans and FFEL Loans when you fail to make your required monthly payments for 270 days. If you have a Perkins Loan, you're in default when you fail to make a payment when due or you fail to comply with your agreement.

When you default on your Direct Loans or FFEL Loans, or both, consolidate or rehabilitate those loans quickly. If you don't, you'll soon find out just how gangsta the Department of Education can be. Not only can it damage your credit score, but it can also garnish your wages, take your tax refund, and take your federal benefits all without suing you. And oh yeah, if it wants, the Department can sue you too.

Consolidation

Getting a Direct Consolidation Loan is the fastest way to get out of default on your federal student loans. After you've consolidated your defaulted loans, you'll no longer be in default and you'll stop collection efforts against you from continuing. You'll also regain your eligibility for financial aid and you'll likely make only one federal student loan payment each month.

Those are the benefits.

There are a few drawbacks. First, the total amount you owe will increase because collection fees will be added to your consolidation loan. Those fees can be up to 18.5% of the loan balance. Second, while the status of your loans on your credit report will state that your defaulted loans were paid in full, the defaulted status will remain. Third, if you have a Perkins Loan, you'll lose cancellation rights. Fourth, if you have a Parent PLUS Loan, consolidating that loan with your other non-PLUS Loans may stop you from repaying the consolidation loan under the income-based-repayment plan. Finally, you usually have only one shot at consolidation. You typically cannot reconsolidate a Direct Consolidation Loan. Because of that, you can only consolidate your way out of default once.

You can't consolidate a defaulted loan that has an active administrative wage garnishment order in place. Likewise, you can't consolidate a defaulted loan that's been reduced to judgment. But if the garnishment order is lifted or the judgment is vacated, you can consolidate that loan.

◆ In his testimony before the U.S. Senate's Special Committee on Aging, Charles A. Jeszeck, Director of Education, Workforce, and Income Security testified that you must be at least 425 days late on your payments before collection attempts such as an administrative wage garnishment or lawsuit are initiated.

Rehabilitation

Although it works much more slowly than does consolidation, federal student loan rehabilitation also allows you to get your loans out of default. By choosing to rehabilitate your defaulted student loan, you're agreeing to make nine timely payments over a 10-month period.

There are at least four benefits of rehabilitation. First, successfully rehabilitating your student loan will remove the default notation from your credit report. That removal doesn't do you much good because the negative payment history will remain. In theory, you can negotiate with your lender to have the negative history removed from your report. But I have yet to see that happen.

Second, you'll keep those Perkins Loan cancellation rights you would've lost if you would have consolidated your loans. Third, you'll stop (and eventually remove) an administrative wage garnishment. This takes at least five timely, monthly payments. Fourth, you'll stop your tax refund from being taken. Finally, you'll regain your eligibility to enroll in income-driven-repayment plans and to receive additional federal student aid.

There are two drawbacks. First, it takes a while to get out of default. With your Direct Loans and your FFEL Loans you have to make nine monthly payments within a 10 month period. (You have only nine months under the Perkins Loan program.) Second, the payments you make under the rehabilitation program likely won't reduce your principal. Your payments are applied first to collection fees, then to interest, and only then are they applied to the principal. Because your rehabilitation payments can be as low as $5, there will likely be nothing left to go toward principal.

Contact your loan holder to reach a rehabilitation agreement. That agreement will define your monthly payment amount and the payment due dates. Your loan holder will calculate your monthly payment using information you provide about your financial status.

Initially, your monthly payment will be calculated by looking at how much you'd pay under the income-based-repayment plan using your most recent tax return. (Remember, under that plan your payment would be 15% of your discretionary income.) If you're earning less than you did last year, submit other proof of your wages using the alternative documentation of income form.

◆ Just because your loan holder looks to the IBR plan to determine your reasonable and affordable payment amount, doesn't mean you're eligible for income-based-repayment. Until you rehabilitate your student loans, you remain in default. And that makes you ineligible for IBR (or any of the other income-driven-repayment plans).

If you can't afford the payment amount your holder initially presents, object to that amount. You may be able to get a reasonable and affordable payment. To get that payment, you'll have to provide additional income and expense information using the financial disclosure for reasonable and affordable rehabilitation payments form.

After you reach an agreement, you must be given a copy of that agreement within 15 days. You'll make the first of your nine payments shortly after you get that copy. So you know, you must make your first payment — and the eight payments after that — within 20 days of its due date. If you don't, your payment is late and that month's payment won't count towards rehabilitation.

CHAPTER 10

When you default on your federal student loans you activate the government's collection powers. And the government has more power than Exar Kun.

Hyperbole? Sure. But not really.

Unlike private student lenders, the government has many options to get its money from you when you fail to pay as agreed. And it doesn't have to go to court to use its powers, which include garnishing your wages, taking your tax refund, taking your federal benefits, and suing you.

I'm assuming you're reading this section because one (or more) of these things is happening to you or is about to happen to you and you want to know what to do. Because of that assumption, I will go into greater detail in this section.

But before I do that, let me hit you with this disclaimer: before trying any of this on your own, sit down with a lawyer. Protect yourself. Protecting yourself probably won't cost you anything. There's likely a student loan lawyer near you who will meet with you for a free consultation. (You can also contact me but I don't do free consultations. As Heath Ledger's Joker said, "If you're good at something, never do it for free."

Administrative wage garnishment

There are few things worse in life than getting a letter from your HR department stating that your next pay check will be garnished for your defaulted federal student loans. Getting that letter is not only embarrassing, but it also triggers the immediate concern of how in the hell are you going to pay your rent and other bills when your check is short 15%?

Your ability to stop your wages from being garnished depends on whether you got notice before or after the Department of Education issued the administrative wage garnishment order.

By law, you're supposed to get notice at least 30 days before the garnishment's start date. Borrowers routinely don't get that notice, however. That's usually because the notice is mailed to the borrower's last known address which, depending on when she last updated it, could be her campus address.

If you get that notice, you'll find it informs of you of the amount you owe and your right to inspect and copy records, enter into a repayment agreement, and request a hearing.

Assuming you get that notice, act quickly. You want to act quickly because if you request a hearing within 30 days of getting the notice, your garnishment shouldn't start until after your hearing date (if it starts at all). But if you wait until after the 30th day, your garnishment will start even though you have a hearing pending.

For now, let's assume you got notified in time to act. What do you do then?

Before the administrative wage garnishment starts

If you act quickly after getting the notice, you can stop the garnishment from starting by requesting a hearing or by entering into a voluntary repayment agreement. You can also stop it by getting out of default through consolidation or rehabilitation or by settling the debt. And if none appeal to you, you can always temporarily stop it by filing for bankruptcy.

Your situation controls which of these garnishment stopping methods you should choose. So you have an idea of how each works, let me explain each one to you.

Voluntary hearing

Mail a request for a hearing to the Department within 30 days after the date on the notice. As of 6 April 2015, the address for submitting your hearing request form is: US Department of Education, Attn: AWG Hearings Branch, PO Box 5227, Greenville TX 75403-5227.

On that request form, you can notify the Department you object to the rate of the garnishment because the garnishment would be a financial hardship to you and your dependents. The Department requires you complete a financial disclosure statement when you object to the garnishment as a hardship.

Besides objecting to the garnishment on hardship grounds, you can also raise several defenses, including:

o   you've been continuously employed for less than a year after you were fired;
o   you're repaying your loan as required by a repayment agreement;

- you don't owe the debt because you never borrowed the loan;
- you don't owe on your student loan because you repaid it;
- you filed for bankruptcy and your case is still open;
- you debt was discharged in bankruptcy;
- you're totally and permanently disabled;
- your school failed to pay you a refund it owed you; or
- you're eligible to discharge your loans because your school closed or your school falsely certified you were eligible for federal aid.

Voluntary repayment agreement

By entering into a voluntary repayment agreement, you're agreeing to pay 15% of your disposable pay. Because that 15% is the same amount that can be taken out by garnishment, the only reason you should reach this agreement with the Department is if your payments are counted towards a rehabilitation plan. (I guess another would be if you wanted to avoid the embarrassment of your employer learning that your wages are being garnished.)

Consolidation + Rehabilitation

Consolidating and rehabilitating your student loans can stop the garnishment from happening by getting you out of default. Because you only get one shot at both consolidation and rehabilitation, be careful. By defaulting on your loans again, you risk placing yourself between the devil and the deep blue sea in trying to repay your loans.

Bankruptcy

Filing bankruptcy will temporarily stop the garnishment from starting. And depending on your situation, you might even discharge your loans in your bankruptcy. It's hard to do. But it can be done.

The drawback to filing bankruptcy to stop your garnishment from starting is that you must get your loans out of default before your bankruptcy completes. (That can be three months to 5 years depending on what bankruptcy chapter you file under.) When your bankruptcy ends, there's nothing stopping the garnishment from starting if you don't get your loans out of default. So develop a plan while your bankruptcy is pending.

Settlement

You can stop the garnishment if you settle your student loan debt. Settlement isn't an option for most borrowers, however. That's because the Department usually doesn't significantly discount the settlement. You'll typically have to present the Department with a lump sum payment of at least 90% of your principal and interest to get it to accept your offer.

Chances are that if you have enough money to settle your student loans you would've been repaying your loans instead of defaulting on them. (But hey, maybe you just inherited the money or went on an Alan Garner type run at the blackjack table.)

After an administrative wage garnishment starts

Consolidation is no longer an option once the garnishment starts. It's prohibited if you have a garnishment in place. You can remove that prohibition, however, if you can lift the garnishment.

Although consolidation is no longer an option, you still can:

- object to the garnishment as a financial hardship;
- rehabilitate your student loans; or
- stop the garnishment temporarily by filing bankruptcy.

Financial hardship

You may object to the rate or amount of the garnishment if you have a financial hardship. And you may object at any time. But if your wages are already being garnished, you must wait at least six months from when the garnishment began before you can object unless your circumstances changed substantially (divorce, injury, sever illness etc.) after you got notice of the garnishment.

When you object, you must submit a hearing request form to the Department of Education. On the first page of the form you'll check the box stating that you're objecting "on the grounds that garnishment in amounts equal to 15% of your disposable pay would cause financial hardship to you and your dependents."

You'll also have to complete a financial disclosure statement. That statement asks for your current income and monthly expenses. Provide as much documentation as possible to support your objection.

Submit the request for hearing form and financial disclosure statement to the Department at: US Department of Education, Attn: AWG Hearings Branch, PO Box 5227, Greenville TX 75403-5227.

The Department will usually decide whether to grant your request within 60 days. Your objection should be granted if you show that you cannot meet your own basic living expenses and those of your dependents.

Unless its review takes longer than 60 days, the Department will keep garnishing your wages while it reviews your request.

Rehabilitation

Because your garnished wages don't count as voluntary payments for rehabilitation, you can rehabilitate your defaulted loan by making payments on top of the garnishment. Sometimes you may be able to subtract your monthly rehabilitation payment from your monthly garnishment amount. There's no guarantee that will happen. But in your situation, asking doesn't hurt.

The garnishment will be suspended after your fifth rehabilitation payment.

Bankruptcy

Filing bankruptcy will temporarily stop the garnishment from starting. And depending on your situation, you might even discharge your loans in your bankruptcy. It's hard to do. But it can be done.

The drawback to filing bankruptcy to stop your garnishment from starting is that you must get your loans out of default before your bankruptcy completes. (That can be three months to 5 years depending on what bankruptcy chapter you file under.) When your bankruptcy ends, there's nothing stopping the garnishment from starting if you don't get your loans out of default.

AWG Extra

The procedures used for garnishing your wages depends on who is collecting the defaulted loan. If it's the Department of Education, then the Department will follow the procedures consistent with the Debt Collection Improvement Act of 1996. But if it's a guaranty agency, then that agency will follow the procedures prescribed under the Higher Education Act. In this section, I focus on when the Department of Education collects. For information on garnishment under the HEA, go to tateesq.com/garnishment-under-HEA.

Tax refund offset

I know, I know. You read through Baller Alert's post on 10 things you can do with your tax refund check (http://bit.ly/1IQjL1B) and had your heart set on fanning them Benjamin's and Instagramming that money for your friends. But then the Department of Education came through like it was the Grinch and you was a resident of Who-ville. Snatched your refund; crushed your dreams. And did it all with no empathy.

If you've defaulted on your federal student loans, the Department can snatch your refund (sometimes called a tax interception or tax offset). And the only thing it has to do before it does that is to send you notice. You may not get that notice though. That's because the Department sends the notice to the last address it has on record for you. So if you've moved since your last update, you won't get that notice.

♦ Worried that your refund may be offset? Call the Program at 800.304.3107 to learn if the Department (or any other federal or state agency) plans to take your refund.

If you get the notice, you'll find you have both an opportunity to inspect your loan records and an opportunity to challenge the taking by submitting a request for review to the Department. Here are some of the defenses to challenge the offset.

You repaid the loan;

o You don't owe the money;
o You've already entered into a repayment agreement with the loan holder and are making the required payments;
o You filed for bankruptcy and your case is still open or your student loans were discharged;
o Your school failed to pay you an owed refund;
o Your loan isn't enforceable because of forgery or other act;
o You're eligible to discharge your loans because your school closed or your school falsely certified you were eligible for federal aid; or
o You're totally and permanently disabled (or the borrower is dead).

By requesting the review you'll temporarily stop your tax refund from being taken. But if you want it to stop permanently, you have three options:

1. Enter into a written agreement to repay your student loans;
2. Consolidate your student loans; or
3. Rehabilitate your student loans.

You can convince the Department to agree not to take your tax refund by entering into a repayment agreement. Request that agreement within 20 days of getting notice that your tax refund will be taken. Your payment is controlled by what the Department's Secretary finds acceptable. But that control shouldn't stop you for asking for a payment that's reasonable and affordable.

Consolidating your student loans will allow you to skip past having to enter into a repayment agreement. Assuming your defaulted loans are eligible, consolidation will get you out of default quickly and it will stop your tax refund from being offset. New loan. No default. Keep refund. Simple.

Another simple step you can take to get out of default and keep your refund is to rehabilitate your defaulted loans. Rehabilitation takes at least nine months. You might want to wait until after you make your ninth payment before you file your tax return. (You'll have to request an extension to late file your return so you don't run afoul of IRS regulations.)

Tax offset extras

Filing bankruptcy before your tax refund is taken triggers an automatic stay. That stay stops the Department from your taking your return. And if you file shortly after your refund is taken, you may get it back under the Bankruptcy Code's provisions concerning preference, post-petition transfer, and setoff actions. Regardless if you file bankruptcy before or after your refund is taken, you still may lose some of your refund to repay your creditors. Many bankruptcy courts will allow you to keep your Earned Income Tax Credit. Speak with a bankruptcy attorney in your area to see if you can keep yours.

The Department can offset the tax refund of joint filing couples. But the portion of the refund owed to the spouse not in default can be recovered by that spouse. The spouse can recover that money by filing an injured spouse claim with the IRS.

Federal benefit offset

The Department of Education's ability to snatch a portion of your monthly Social Security benefits check is the gangster-est of all its collection powers. That power is more gangsta than all of those Thug Life meme's combined. Yes, even the one with President Obama letting his haters know he has no more races to run.

I say it's the most powerful because Social Security benefits aren't considered income under the income-driven-repayment plans. So if most of your monthly money comes from those benefits, your payment under one of the IDR plans would be zero. This result means that the Department can take money that but for your default it wouldn't otherwise be able to take.

Now that's powerful.

To be fair, there are some limits on that power. For instance, besides Social Security benefits, the only other federal benefits the Department can take a portion of are benefits under Part B of the Black Lung Act and some Railroad Retirement benefits.

And even that power has two limitations. First, the Department can take a piece of those benefits only if you get more than $9 thousand per year. So if you only get $750 per month (which equals $9 thousand per year) in non-exempt federal benefits, the Department can't take it. Second, the Department can offset no more than 15% of your annual benefit.

You can stop the Department from taking that much by requesting a hardship reduction. You can use the financial hardship claim self-help packet provided by the Student Loan Borrower Assistance Project to help prepare your request. Get the packet at: http://bit.ly/1FtQ2IV.

Two other options to stop your benefits from being offset are to reach a repayment agreement with the Department or file for bankruptcy. While reaching a repayment agreement permanently stops your benefits from being taken, filing bankruptcy only temporarily stops your benefits from being taken. Choose whichever options works best for you.

Lawsuit

The Department of Education rarely sues borrowers to collect federal student loans. It has so many other powers it can use outside of court (administrative wage garnishment, tax return offset, and federal benefits offset) suing to collect rarely makes sense.

But because it has the power to sue, the Department can use that power whenever it wants. (There's no statute of limitations.) And it usually uses that power against self-employed people who don't receive tax refunds. Why those borrowers? Because the government has no way to seize the money from them. It's not like self-employed people are going to garnish their own wages.

There's one simple rule you need to remember if the government ever sues you: don't ignore the lawsuit. Answer the lawsuit. And if you can afford it, hire a student loan attorney to protect your interest.

Depending on your situation, your attorney (or if you represent yourself) may have several defenses for your nonpayment to choose from, including:

o   You made payments to the lender that weren't credited to your account;
o   You're current on your account;
o   You don't owe the debt;
o   You don't owe the amount due; (Sometimes your lender will ask for attorney's fees or collections costs that are either too high or aren't allowed by law.);
o   Your lender's trying to collect more than you agreed to pay; or
o   You discharged the debt in bankruptcy.

You may also have a defense if you believe the loan isn't enforceable due to forgery, mistake, fraud, or some other reason.

While your case is pending, you can try to negotiate a payment plan or reduced settlement amount with the Department of Education. (The Department has authority to compromise (settle) FFEL Loans and Perkins Loans.) The Department may settle your federal student loan debt by agreeing to waive collection charges; cutting 10% from the total owed; or settling for the current principal owed plus half the accrued interest.

If you can't reach an agreement with the Department and you lose the lawsuit, the court will enter a judgment against you. That judgment gives your lender the right to force you to pay using different tools. The effectiveness of these tools depends on how much income and property you have.

If you're judgment proof, there's not much that can be done to you. Federal and state laws protect your assets and income from seizure. But you'll only be protected if your assets and income stay small. If they ever increase, you may have to repay the judgment.

CHAPTER 11

Unless you won your state's lottery, inherited money from your great uncle Rupert Horn, or were a Shark Tank success story, you likely don't have the means to settle your student loan debt.

But if you have the extra cash lying around —your 401k? — you have the option to settle your FFEL Loans or your Perkins Loans for less than you owe. Admittedly, settling your loans is hard to do. And it's even harder to do if you're current on your loan payment. But hard doesn't mean impossible.

There are two types of settlements you can offer the Department: a standard compromise or a discretionary compromise. Standard compromises can either be to waive your collection charges, settle for your current principal balance plus half of your accrued but unpaid interest, or settle for at least 90% of your current principal and interest balance.

Here are examples of the three standard compromises:

1. **Waiver of collection costs**. You owe $2500 in principal, $1 thousand in interest, and $875 in projected collection fees. The collector may accept a settlement as low as $3500.00 (principal and interest) to satisfy the account.
2. **Principal and half interest**. You owe $2 thousand in principal, $1 thousand in interest, and $730.20 in projected collection costs. The collector can accept a settlement as low as $2,500.00 (principal + 50% interest) to satisfy the account.
3. **90% principal and interest**. You owe $2 thousand in principal, $400 in interest and $584.16 projected collection costs. The

collector can accept a settlement as low as $2160.00 (90% of principal + interest) to satisfy the account.

If you want to offer anything less than one of those amounts, your offer is a discretionary compromise. It's discretionary because the Department must approve your offer. (That's in contrast to the standard compromise, which the Department has given a sort of preapproval for.)

When you submit your discretionary compromise offer, you must also submit a letter justifying your offer. And if you're offering a discretionary compromise because of a financial hardship, you must provide information about your income and expenses.

Once the Department approves your compromise, you'll have up to 90 days to make your payment if you request that much time. If you don't request that much time, you'll likely have only 20 days to make your payment. Any payments made after your deadline likely won't count and your settlement will likely be voided.

Settling your debt for less than you owe may have tax consequences for you. That's because the difference between what you owed and what you paid may be considered taxable income. Contact a tax professional to address your tax questions.

CHAPTER 12

Because PLUS loans don't allow a cosigner to be released from their obligation, the only way that I know of to get a cosigner released is to refinance with a private lender. And depending on your situation, the refinanced loan might also require a cosigner. But if you're desperate to get your cosigner released, the key thing to do is to make certain that the terms of the refinance loan allow your cosigner to be released after a set number of payments.

Does getting a cosigner removed from a PLUS Loan seem circuitous? Yes.

The question though is should you do it? I have yet to arrive at a good answer.

========================

PART II
PRIVATE STUDENT LOANS

========================

Private student loans suck. Somewhere 2-Chainz just yelled, "Trueeeee." Private student lenders and their poor customer service and poorer loan products make me want to snap on them like Quagmire snapped on Brian. I hope they always have snow in their driveways. I hope they never get off Fridays and they have to work at a Friday's that's busy every Friday. (Hat tip Chance the Rapper and his verse in Action Bronson's Baby Blue.)

Seriously though, private student loans are just terrible. Except that time when you really needed them when you were in school because you spent all of your federal student aid on books, laptop, sneakers, dates, food, alcohol, and road trips. (And not necessarily in that order.) When you needed them, private student loans were the greatest thing since Flaming Hot Cheetos smothered in ground beef and cheese sauce.

But just like we found out years later that Flaming Hots might have been killing us all along (http://trib.in/1aQoPIK) so too did we find out after we got out of school that private student loans were the absolute devil.

Have you tried getting your lender to give you a lower monthly payment on your private student loan? For some of you, getting that payment was harder to do than getting an extra pack of soy sauce with your fried rice. (That last line is a reference to a bit from comedian DL Hughley: http://bit.ly/1ybGNj5.)

Unlike your federal student loans, you typically can't get a payment based on your income. You typically can't get your loans forgiven just because you work for the government or a 501(c)(3). And you typically can't get them forgiven because you're dead. When it comes to getting that money, private student lenders are Stewie and you're Brian. (Watch Stewie's beat down of Brian here: http://bit.ly/1bSonHZ.)

Despite their general lack of flexible repayment plans and forgiveness options, private student loans do have some advantages when it comes time for repayment. First, unlike federal student loans, private student loans are subject to your state's statute of limitations. Second, private student lenders have less collection powers then the government has when you default on your loans. Third, private student loans may be negotiated for a lower settlement percentage than federal loans. Finally, depending on what school you went to when you borrowed your private loans, you might have a greater chance of getting those loans discharged than you would with your federal student loans.

That last advantage refers to a specific provision — 11 U.S.C. § 523(a)(8)(B) — in the Bankruptcy Code that prescribes hurdles that private student loans must jump to be considered nondischargeable. Because discharging your student loans in bankruptcy is outside this book's scope, I'm not going to discuss that bankruptcy provision further. You can check tateesq.com/qualified-education-loans for more information.

The easiest way to tell if your student loans are private is to check the National Student Loan Data System. (There's no similar system for private student loans.) That System has all of your federal student loans. So if you have a loan and it's not listed, then the loan is private.

Another way to find your private student loans is to check your credit reports. Your private student loans should be listed.

Choosing a repayment plan for your private student loans is totally different than it is for your federal student loans. With your private loans, you don't choose whether you want to repay your loans in 10 years or 30 years and you don't have income-driven-repayment options either. Without your lender's mercy, you're stuck paying your loan according to the terms in the promissory note you signed.

When a lender does offer its mercy, it typically does so in the form of interest only payments for a period usually lasting no more than 18 months. To get approved for that payment plan you typically have to provide (over the phone or in writing) your personal financial statement. That statement includes your monthly income and expenses and the amounts in your checking, savings, and retirement accounts.

To get information from your lender about alternative repayment options, send your lender a letter asking about those options. The Consumer Financial Protection Bureau has a sample letter you can use.

◆ If you're wondering why your private student lenders offer few repayment options, it's because they aren't allowed to. Read more at: http://bit.ly/1lt6YWX.

◆ You may have more success in getting an alternative payment plan if you're in default on your private student loans. Your default status may also make available loan medication and settlement options. (Modification is generally available if you're suffering a long term hardship.)

CHAPTER 16

Your ability to defer or forbear your private student lender varies from lender to lender. Private lenders aren't obligated to offer you these options to temporarily stop your repayment. It's their discretion. Some lenders will use their discretion while you're in school but won't use it afterwards. And other lenders will grant you a short term forbearance if you provide evidence that you have the ability and the desire to repay your private student loans in the future.

Contact your private student lender to get information about placing your loans in deferment or forbearance.

CHAPTER 17

Whether you should refinance your private student loans depends on your ability to secure a new loan that has an interest rate lower than the one you have now. As with other installment consumer debts such as a mortgage or car loan, you'd want to refinance your loan if you can get a rate that's materially less than what you're currently paying so that you pay less over the life of the loan. That's just good financial sense.

But your ability to get that refi-loan may depend on things like your credit score (at least 660) and history, your level of education, your collegiate alma mater, your employment history, your yearly wages, and your occupation. And even if all that information makes you worthy of a refi-loan, the refinancing lender still may request you get a cosigner who is at least equally credit worthy.

If you're interested in refinancing your private student loans, check out these companies:

- SoFi;
- CommonBond;
- Citizens Financial Group;
- Discover Financial Services;
- LendKey;
- CordiaGrad; and
- Darien Rowayton Bank.

Some private lenders will allow you to refinance or consolidate your federal student loans with your private student loans.

Before you decided to convert your federal student loan into a private student loan, consider all that you might be giving up in exchange for a lower interest rate. You'll lose income-driven-repayment options, prescribed deferment and forbearance periods, and certain forgiveness and cancellation rights.

♦ If you want more information on refinancing your private student loans, Reddit has an informative thread with people sharing their private student loan refinancing stories.

CHAPTER 18

Historically, private student lenders rarely cancel (forgive) student loans. There are a few lenders, however, who have begun offering borrowers an opportunity to have their loans cancelled. For example, Sallie Mae offers total and permanent disability cancellation on its Smart Option Student Loans and it has also said that it would forgive any unpaid balance at the primary borrower's death.

As of now, the borrower's death and disability are the only routine instances I know of where a private student loan lender is cancelling loans.

The standards for getting your private student loans forgiven for disability vary from lender to lender. That said, some lenders do follow the federal disability discharge guidelines.

CHAPTER 19

Let's keep this section short: to avoid defaulting on your private student loans pay them on time or place them in deferment or forbearance. (That's if you can get either of those two options.)

But if you can't avoid defaulting — generally you're in default when your loans are 120 days past due — you'll face two consequences: your credit score will take a hit and your lender will have the right to sue you to try and collect on the loan.

◆ You could also default on your loan by dying, breaking a promise in your promissory note, filing for bankruptcy (you or your cosigner), becoming insolvent, or providing a false written statement to your lender. Depending on your promissory note, your default may trigger your lender's right to immediately demand the balance due on your loan.

Defaulting on your private student loans doesn't have the same consequences as defaulting on your federal loans. Compared to the government, private lenders have few collection powers. Indeed, they have only two: (1) demanding payment from you using phone calls and letters and (2) suing you to try and get a judgment so it can attempt to garnish your wages and place a lien on your real property.

If your lender decides to sue you, it must be do so within a certain number of years after you default. Your state's statute of limitations prescribes that number of years.

And not only does your lender have to sue you within a certain number of years, if it wins that lawsuit, it has a certain number of years to try and enforce that win. Your state also prescribes that number of years.

All isn't lost if you lose that lawsuit. Depending on your income, you may be able to take advantage of your state's exemption laws. Those exemption laws stop your lender from collecting from you so long as you meet the requirements.

Contact a student loan attorney in your state to learn more about your state's statute of limitations and exemption laws.

CHAPTER 21

There's no one formula or procedure for settling your private student loans. Each lender handles settlement offers in its own way. That said, no matter who your lender is, the success of your settlement offer will likely be affected by two things: whether you're in default and whether you can pay a lump sum shortly after your settlement offer is accepted. (In some extreme cases, you can get a couple of years to pay the settlement amount.)

As for how much you'll have to pay in a lump sum, there's no one number. No one percentage. You can expect that if a settlement is reached, the amount will be for somewhere between 40% and 85% of the principal balance owed.

◆ You can learn more about people who successfully settled their debt with a particular lender by searching reddit.com. That site has plenty of stories from people who say they settled their student loans with Sallie Mae, Navient, Wells Fargo, and others. Here's the search string I use in Google Chrome to search Reddit for that information: "site:reddit.com private student loan settlement".

If you reach a settlement, get a written agreement stating that your payment will cause the loan to be paid in full.

CHAPTER 22
GETTING A COSIGNER RELEASED

At some point you got to let your cosigner off the hook for your private student loan debt. It's the right thing to do.

Many lenders will allow this to be done after a set number of payments have been made and you (assuming you're the primary borrower) have obtained a satisfactory credit score, job, and income. To find out the qualifications for getting your cosigner released (or if you're the cosigner, getting yourself released) send your lender a letter asking for that information.

The Consumer Financial Protection Bureau has a letter you can use if you're the primary borrower or if you're the cosigner. Get the letter here: http://1.usa.gov/1ixVnZj.

The standard for getting a release varies from lender to lender. You can expect, however, that you (or whomever the primary borrower is) will have to make at least 24 consecutive, timely, monthly payments before a cosigner release will be granted.

There is no one answer on what to do with your private student loans. Your answer depends on your loans, your finances, your facts. Instead of telling you what to do, let me share with you the process I go through with each of my clients.

1. Have the client record her monthly income and expenses.
2. Identify and record all private student loans.
3. Request a copy of the promissory note for each loan.
4. Review the promissory note, checking for any promises made by the lender and any deferment, forbearance, cancellation (or forgiveness), or alternative repayment plan terms.
5. Depending on the client's situation, I'll contact their private student loan lender to either: (a) negotiate a settlement; (b) negotiate a cosigner release; (c) request an interest rate reduction or loan modification, or both; (d) request a deferment or forbearance; or (e) request an alternative repayment plan.

Now that I've shared my process with you, allow me to walk you through each step in that process.

Recording monthly income + expenses

Recording your monthly income and expenses provides a snapshot of not only where money is going but also whether there's a need to request a deferment, forbearance, or an alternative repayment plan.

There are two benefits of recording income and expenses. First, it puts your financial health in perspective. Second, it prepares you to answer the same questions your private student loan lender will ask if you request a settlement, cosigner release, or alternative repayment plan.

Identifying private student loans

With all the money you borrowed over the years to pay for your education it can be hard to remember who you borrowed from. If you can't remember which of your loans are federal or private, the easiest thing to do is to check the Department of Education's National Student Loan Data System. That system only contains federal student loans. So if you got a bill from a lender that's not listed in the System, chances are you have a private student loan with that lender.

You can also find out if your loan is private by checking the loan's interest rate. Any student loan with an interest rate higher than 8.5% is private.

Another tip off your loan is private is if there's a cosigner. Only Direct PLUS loans require a cosigner. So if you have a loan with a cosigner and it's not a PLUS loan, your loan is likely private.

After you've identified which of your loans are private, record them on a log to track, among other things, who the loan is with, who is servicing the loan, how much is owed, and what's the loan's interest rate. Doing this makes it easier to later develop a plan of action for each loan.

Request a copy of the note

Once I know which private lenders my client has loans with, I send those lenders a letter requesting a copy of the promissory note. In my experiences, lenders usually take about two to three weeks to send the note. Here's a sample request letter.

Review the note

After I get the note I check to see:

o Whether my client signed the note and on what date;
o What promises the lender has made;
o When may my client request a deferment, forbearance, or alternative repayment plan;
o When may any cosigner be released from her obligation; and
o What events allow for the loan to be cancelled or forgiven.

Contact the lender for payment options

The promissory note usually doesn't say much about alternative repayment options. And aside from mentioning an in school deferment, the note might not mention the ability to request a deferment or forbearance.

I usually have to contact each lender to get that information. You can use this letter from the Consumer Financial Protection Bureau to get that information.

When I get a lender's response, here's what I typically find.

Deferment and forbearance

Many private student loan lenders offer deferments or short term forbearances. In either instance, they ask for evidence supporting the request. That evidence must show that you can and are willing to repay the loan.

Repayment options

Depending on your financial situation, your lender may be willing to lower your interest rate (temporarily or permanently), waive all accrued interest, lower your monthly payment (temporarily or permanently), or settle your loan for a portion of what you owe.

In my experience, when it comes to doing anything permanently with your loan (lowering interest rate, waiving accrued interest, lowering monthly amount, settling, etc.) your lender is less willing to work with you when you're current. When you're delinquent, your lender wants to get money flowing again. And this is good business for them not just in terms of having money coming in, but also on the evaluation of their loan portfolio. In (very) simplistic terms, the fewer delinquent loans they have in their portfolio, the better their credit rating.

◆ If you're planning on financing a home or car, you might benefit from putting your private student loans (and for that matter, your federal student loans) in deferment or forbearance. The reason is that if your monthly payments are no longer due, your debt to income ratio has decreased, leaving you with more discretionary income to contribute towards a loan. Granted, this is a temporary fix. At some point, you're going to have to deal with your student loans.

===================

**PART II
MONEY**

===================

In reality, for some of you, there's not much you can do to get rid of your federal student loans or your private student loans any quicker. If you don't qualify for one of the federal student loan forgiveness programs, it might take you decades to pay those off. And forgiveness for your private student loans doesn't exist. So if you can't get your loans forgiven, what can you do to get rid of them quicker?

Here are 13 tips to help you do that.

1. **Make larger payments**. For example, a $25 thousand student loan with 6.8% interest with a 10-year payback period would cost $288 per month. Paying $700 a month would shrink your payback period to just over three years.
2. **Pay bi-weekly**. If you pay bi-weekly, you'll pay less in interest because there's less time for interest to accrue. And you'll also make an extra month's payment every year. That's because paying bi-weekly equals 26 annual payments, which is 13 monthly payments.
3. **Use your tax refund**. After you use the tax deduction you get for paying student loan interest (up to $2500) use your refund to pay off some of your student loans.
4. **Refinance your loans**. You may be able to drop your interest rate 4% by refinancing your federal or private student loans, or both. SoFi, for instance, starts their fixed interest rates at 3.9% and their variable interest rates at 1.9% APR (with auto debit).

There are dangers in refinancing your federal student loans. For example, your new private student loan may not have income driven repayment plans and may not be forgiven when you die, leaving your estate liable for your student loan debt.

5. **Enroll in auto debit**. By enrolling in auto debit you'll get a .25% interest rate deduction. (Navient offers this deduction.) You'll also never miss a payment. And that's a good thing if you're trying to forgive your loans under the Public Service Loan Forgiveness program.
6. **Hustle**. You can bring in extra money to repay your student loans by getting a side hustle. Sites such as gogirlfinance.com, moneyunder30.com, and thecollegeinvestor.com have a lengthy list of ideas for side hustling your way out student loan debt.
7. **Use tech**. Financial technology companies such as Gradible allow you to do various internet based tasks such as posting to Facebook and Craigslist in exchange for earning money ($10–$15 hour) paid directly to your student loan lender. Other Fintech companies such as Achieve Lending and Credible allow you to compare interest rates on private student loans in seconds.
8. **Volunteer**. In exchange for volunteering, you can get money for your loans. Here are organizations you can volunteer with:

- SponsorChange;
- Volunteers in Service to America;
- AmeriCorps;
- PeaceCorps;
- Teach for America;
- National Health Service Corps; and
- Army National Guard.

9. **Move**. You can get help repaying your student loan payments just by moving to certain places. Here are places where this is happening.

- *Rural Kansas*. Get up to $15 thousand for living in a rural zone of Kansas for five years.
- *Niagara Falls*. Get $7 thousand toward your student loans by living in the Falls for two years.
- *Saskatchewan Canada*. Get up to $20 thousand for living in Saskatchewan.

10. **Use credit rewards**. Cash in sign up bonuses. For example, the Chase Ink Plus card offers a signup bonus of 70 thousand points after spending $5 thousand in three months. You can cash those points out and get $700 each time you do.
11. **Get a monthly repayment as a gift**. When your friends and family ask you what you want for a birthday, holiday, or graduation gift, tell them to make one of your student loan payments for you. One company, tuition.io, has developed an online platform that allows your friends and family to gift you anywhere from $5–$500 for your student loans.
12. **Enroll in Upromise**. This option only works if you have student loans with Sallie Mae. Upromise works by giving you a percentage of cash back for shopping online using Upromise's links. The money returned to you is applied directly toward your loans with Sallie Mae. You can even get your family and friends to register to increase how much money is applied to your debt.
13. **Sell eggs, sperm, and more**. Although some might find selling bits of their self-offensive, others will do it to repay their student loans. Some women have gotten $10 thousand an egg. Meanwhile, men command about $1500 per month for their donated sperm. And at least one man has sold his testicle, collecting $35 thousand in the process.

But what if $1500 to $10 thousand doesn't cover your student loan debt? Well, if you're a woman, consider renting out your womb for 10 months or auctioning your virginity. Surrogate mothers get about $25 thousand, and a virginity auction got one woman $3.9 million for her virginity.

My goal in sharing this particular information isn't to suggest you should rent your womb or have you impregnate dozens of women like She Hate Me's John Henry Armstrong to repay your student loans. My only goal was to share with you legal options others have pursued.

But seriously though $3.9 million for virginity? To think I gave mine up for three cheddar biscuits and a sea food platter. Laughing but so serious.

In my Kevin Hart voice, "Look. Here's the thing about repaying student loans. If you want to get rid of them quickly, you're going to have to get real about your budget." Matter of fact, you're going to have to get a budget.

I know some of your right know are like DC Young Fly and saying: "Budget? Fawk you mean?"

Yeah. A budget.

Shit just got real.

So how do you get your budget?

For most of my clients, we don't even start with developing a budget. Our work begins about 30 days before that. Why 30 days? Answer: how can you accurately budget where your money is going if you don't know how and where you're spending your money?

The accuracy of your budget depends on your ability to answer these how and where questions. That's why I advise my clients to track how much they spend over 30 days.

Admittedly, tracking spending isn't easy to do. It takes preparation. It takes diligence. It takes triggers. But mostly, it takes purpose.

As is true with most things, you're more successful when you have a why. So as Eric Thomas asks his Thank God It's Monday YouTube subscribers: What's your why?

Is it to be debt free by x age? Is it to buy a home? Is it to start saving for retirement? Is it so you can pay for your child's education?

Why do you want to develop a budget?

Once you have that answer, tracking your spending becomes easier. Still not easy. But easier.

If you need a jump start on finding your why, here's what I did to find mine: I asked myself why three times. After I did that, I had my why. Let me show you how those questions worked for me.

1. Why do I want to develop a budget? Because I need to start saving for retirement.
2. Why do I need to start saving for retirement? Because I don't want to have to depend on any one to take care of me.
3. Why don't I want to have to depend on anyone? Because I'm a man and a man takes care of his family; not the other way around.

So what's my why for budgeting? I budget because I'm a man and as a man I have to take care of my family. My family shouldn't have to take care of me.

Is this purpose finding method simplistic and slightly reductive? Absolutely. But getting to your why doesn't have to be a complex, soul searching process. Keep things simple so you get to your why.

Tracking spending

Now that you have your why, let's talk about how to track your spending for the next 30 days. You have two ways to do this: analog and digital.

Analog

Envelope, post notes, + paper. Use the envelope to capture all your receipts during the day. The post notes? Use them to document those things you don't get a receipt for. Vending machine purchases for example. And the paper? Use it as your spending brain; the place where you record all the receipts you accumulated over the month.

Digital

Sheets + apps. Google Sheets should be your go to spreadsheet software for two reasons. First, Sheets is free. Second, you can access Sheets wherever you have an internet connection. That accessibility is key for logging your spending wherever you want, from whatever e device you want.

No matter what spreadsheet program you go with, use simple labels to describe what you spend your money on. You want to make this so easy that you'll keep doing it. So no matter where you get your food from (groceries, take out, vending machines) label your spending as "food" and be done with it. Same thing goes for gas, electric, water, etc. Label that group as utilities and keep it moving.

If spreadsheets aren't your thing, or if you need something right on your phone or tablet, use apps to track your spending.

When choosing a tool or tools to track your spending, keep it simple. By deciding to track your spending you're deciding to build a habit. And the key to building any habit is to make doing it so easy that you can't say no.

Budgeting with the envelope system

After you've tracked your spending for at least 30 days, you're ready to develop a budget. There are a bunch of tools you can use to do this. In fact, there are so many that choosing one can become so difficult that you choose to do nothing.

So let's keep things simple. And the simplest budgeting system I know is the envelope system.

The envelope system is great because it makes budgeting tangible. You take the money you make each paycheck and put them in envelopes that you've pre labeled for certain expenses — "food", "rent", "utilities", and "student loans", for example — and the amount you budgeted for that expense. So for example, your food envelop will be labeled "Food – $200".

Don't worry if you don't make enough each paycheck to cover large expenses such as your rent. That's not a problem. If you get paid bi-weekly, put half of what's needed to cover your rent in the envelope every time you get paid.

Once you've apportioned the money, it's time to spend. And since the money available to spend is controlled by what's left in the envelope, the only way you ever spend more than what you've budgeted is if you take money from elsewhere (bank withdrawals, other envelopes, gifts, etc.) and put it in the envelope. Assuming you stick with what you've budgeted, the envelope systems works well and it's super simple.

The envelope system has four major drawbacks. First, toting all those envelopes around will have you looking like some crazed couponing soccer mom. But who cares. You're budgeting like a rock star.

Second, the envelope system is a bit clunky. It works best with cash. Going to the bank every pay period to withdraw money is a pain. And so too is carrying change in the envelope.

Third, using the envelope system doesn't work (conveniently) for paying your student loans. It's not as if you can visit your local FedLoan Servicing or Navient branch and make a cash payment. Because of that, it might make sense to keep the money you budgeted for your student loans in the bank and setting that money up for auto pay (especially if you get an interest rate reduction for auto payments).

Finally, the envelope system might cause you to pay more for goods. Imagine that you're looking to buy a plane ticket and you find your flight but you don't buy it because you don't have enough money in your travel envelope. So you wait until next month to get the money to buy the ticket. But now when you go to buy it, the ticket is more expensive. In this case, the envelope system doesn't make sense because you were going to spend the money anyway. So buy it when it's the cheapest.

I understand if the envelope system thing isn't for you. Trust me I get it. So if you're interested in other options, check out this terrific post on choosing a budget system written by Trent Hamm, a writer with thesimpledollar.com. You can also get some ideas from Reddit's personal finance page at: http://www.red-dit.com/r/personalfinance/wiki/budgeting.

Methods to repay debt are many. Two of the more popular methods are the Debt Snowball and the Debt Avalanche methods.

The Debt Snowball method

The Debt Snowball method requires you pay your smallest balances first. The thinking behind this is that you create momentum with each debt you pay off. And that momentum will encourage you to keep paying off your debts until none remain.

The first thing you do in this method is list all of your debts in order from the account with the least total balance to the account with the greatest. In all likelihood, when you do this, credit card bills and medical bills will be first on the list and your student loan bills will be somewhere near the middle (or if you're like me) or last on your list. (Yes, I owe more in student loans than I do on my home.) But that's okay. It's okay because the theory behind the Debt Snowball method is that by the time you pay off your accounts with smaller balances, you'll not only have a good deal of cash to throw at your student loans but you'll also have this huge snowball of momentum behind you.

After you've properly ranked your debts, start making minimum payments on all of your debts except the one with the smallest balance. Pay as much as you can toward that debt and keep paying on it until it's gone. After that, sprint to the next one, carrying the money you were putting toward the first with you.

Keep repeating that process until all of your debt is gone, student loans included.

The biggest drawback of this method is the most obvious: by paying attention only to the account with the smallest balance rather than the one with the highest interest rate, you'll likely pay more money in the long run. For that reason many financial advisers advise against using this method. They instead advise you tackle the much more mathematically and financially sound method of paying off your balances with the highest interest rate. Or in other words, those advisers would tell you to use the Debt Avalanche method.

The Debt Avalanche method

Under the Debt Avalanche method you'll pay off your balances with the highest interest first. While the Debt Snowball method appeals to your emotions, the Debt Avalanche method appeals to your logic. It prioritizes efficiency and it is the cheapest and fastest way to get out of debt.

Here's how it works.

You start by ranking your debts from the account with the highest interest rate to the one with the lowest interest rate. For many of my clients, their student loans usually fall towards the bottom of the interest rate list, especially if they don't have private student loans. This is because their accounts with the highest interest rate are usually their credit cards and car notes. (I routinely see interest rates on credit cards and cars over 25%. As Ron Simmons would say, "Damn!")

Now that you've got your debts listed by highest to lowest interest rate, make minimum payments on all your debts except for the one with the highest interest. When it comes to that debt, you want to pay as much as you can so you can get rid of it quickly. Once that debt's gone, move on to the debt with the next highest interest rate. Keep going to all of your debt is gone.

Simple, right?

Despite this method's simplicity, it does have an emotional drawback. Unless your accounts with the highest interest rates have the lowest amount, you may not get rid of your first debt until months after you start on your debt repayment strategy. Do you have the strength to keep pushing to get rid of a debt if it takes you 10 months to pay off the first?

If you do, great. This is the plan for you. But if you don't have that strength or if you're not sure that you do, the Debt Snowball method might be your thing. You'll see wins faster. And that might make all the difference in how soon you get rid of all of your debt, including your student loans.

Final notes on debt payment methods + student loans

If you're like me and your student loan debt is the largest debt you have (or is one of the largest debts you have) and you're going to use the Debt Snowball method, enroll in an income-driven-repayment plan for your federal student loans and look into reducing your monthly private student loan payment.

Reducing your student loan payments lowers your minimum amount due each month on your loans, allowing you to contribute more towards your account with the smallest balance and gets rid of your first debt faster. Yes, depending on how long it takes you to direct your snowball at your student loans, you might owe a stupid amount in interest. But that's okay because you'll likely have enough money to repay your student loans much, much quicker than you would if you still had to pay other debt.

One other method to consider is filing for bankruptcy under chapter 7. Yes, your credit score will take a hit. And yes, you might be ashamed or feel as if you've somehow been defeated by filing for bankruptcy. But setting your credit score and emotions aside, bankruptcy might be the most logical way to get rid of most of your debt quickly.

By filing bankruptcy, you'll be able to aim your snowball or avalanche at your student loans faster than you would under either method. That's because your bankruptcy will eliminate most of your other debt, leaving you only to pay your student loans.

Credit reports and credit scores affect your life. No secret. Credit scores affect your ability to buy a home, car, and a wedding ring. And it also affects your ability to get credit cards and personal loans, including private student loans.

Of all the things affecting your credit, student loans are among those having the most impact. Why? Answer: student loans have a big impact on your credit score because your report will usually be filled with not just one student loan, but several student loans. And each of those loans has its own age, balance owed, and payment history. So the good news is that if you timely pay your student loans, they can have a big positive impact on your score. But the bad news is that they can also have a big negative impact on your score.

So how do you do you maximize your student loans so they positively affect your credit score?

Before getting to that answer, let's start by breaking down the factors that compose your credit score. (Since most creditors use your FICO score, I'll address the factors it uses to determine scores.)

1. **Your payment history (35%)**. Because paying your bills on time has the greatest reward for your credit score, make sure you do that; it says a lot about your personal financial responsibility and creditworthiness.
2. **The amount you owe (30%)**. Keep your balances low compared to the maximum amount allowed. But you don't want a zero

balance. That's because only responsible use of credit —
maintaining a low balance and making monthly payments —
boosts your score.

3. **The length of your credit history (15%)**. Both the age of your
   overall credit history and the age of your individual accounts
   impact your score. You want to establish credit early in life and
   you want your accounts to be old with positive payment
   histories.

4. **Your credit mix (10%)**. You want a mix of revolving credit (credit
   cards) and installment loans (mortgage and auto loan). People
   with strong credit scores usually have a mix of both accounts.

5. **The number of recent hard credit inquiries (10%)**. Every time
   you apply for credit, you generate a hard inquiry on your account.
   That hard inquiry dings your credit score, especially if your overall
   age of credit history is young.

Now that we know what factors compose your credit score (at
least as FICO is concerned), let's discuss how student loans
affect the five factors.

Timely repaying your loans has a huge impact on your score

Here's the good news. Paying your student loans on time
positively impacts your credit score. And so too does placing your
student loans in deferment or forbearance. Both methods of
temporarily stopping your payments appear on your credit report
as "paid as agreed".

The bad news though is that just like any other credit account,
paying your student loan payments late negatively affects your
credit score. But if you have federal student loans, don't trip if
you're late by a day: your federal student loan servicers wait until

you're late by 90 days to report your late payment history to the three major credit bureaus (Equifax, Experian, and Transunion).

Private student loan lenders, on the other hand, report your late payments to the bureaus at different times. Sallie Mae, for instance, waits until you're 45 days late before it reports. Given the difference in reporting time between your federal and private lenders, you may be better off timely paying your private student loan and being late with your federal student loan.

◆ No matter your financial situation, don't let nine months (270 days) go by before you make a payment on your federal student loans. If you do that, you'll be in default, and you'll open yourself up to the government taking your tax return and garnishing your wages, among other things. Plus, defaulting on your student loans is a red flag to your lenders and it makes finding an apartment and getting utilities that much harder (increased security deposit for example).

How much you owe on your student loans has little impact on your credit score

The amount you owe in student loans has little significant effect on your credit score. Why? Student loans are installment loans and installment loan indebtedness is a weak predictor of your future borrowing performance. On the other hand, a revolving type of debt, such as credit card debt, is a strong predictor. That's why it's important to keep the balances you owe on your credit cards low, like less than 20% of the credit limit low.

Although the balance you owe on your student loans has little impact on your credit score, it affects your ability to take out other loans. Mortgage lenders, for example, look at your debt to income ratio. So do car companies. (Your debt to income ratio compares how much total monthly debt payments you make vs. your monthly income.) If your ratio is too high, you might not get the loan. Or if you do, it might be for a higher interest rate.

◆ You may be able to reduce your debt to income ratio by placing your loan in deferment or by switching to an income-driven-repayment plan, which may lower your monthly payments. (The effectiveness of deferment may depend on the loan you're looking to get.) You may also be able to reduce your ratio by refinancing or consolidating your loans, both of which may lower your interest rate while stretching your loan repayment over a longer period.

Student loans are often borrowers first credit account

Often, the only credit accounts on a college aged students' (17 thru 23) report are student loans. The accounts for credit cards, cars, personal loans, and homes, don't appear until after. But by the time you get those accounts, your student loan accounts will be the oldest accounts on your credit report. And that means you need to care for them by making timely payments or requesting deferment or forbearance when necessary.

Student loans add positively to your credit mix

Having a mix of student loan debt (installment debt) and credit card debt (revolving debt) improves your credit score by showing you can handle a wide variety of credit accounts. And not only is it important to have diverse credit accounts, it's also important to have accounts from diverse lenders. In *The Credit Cleanup Book*, author Shindy Chen suggests that your credit score is affected by who your creditor is. So for instance, successfully repaid loans from payday lenders add less value to your credit report than do loans from banks such as Chase or Bank of America.

Limit hard inquiries when getting student loans

Hard inquiries indicate that you're actively trying to get credit. If you're shopping for the best rate on your student loan, try and limit your shopping to a two week period. Doing that will likely cause your multiple inquiries to be treated as one inquiry on your credit report.

Recap

To get the greatest credit score from your student loans you should pay your monthly student loan bills on time, keep your student loan accounts open for a while, get other types of credit (mortgage, auto loan, etc.), and if you're going to shop around for private student loans, do so within a two-week period.

Student loan + credit score extras

Paying off student loans early hurts your credit score a smidge. Paying off your student loans early doesn't affect the age of that account. The only hurt you'll experience is a lost opportunity to steadily improve your credit score by aging those accounts and paying them off over a longer period. The benefit though is that by paying off early you stop accruing interest.

Rehabilitating a defaulted student loan removes the default code. By rehabilitating a student loan, you'll remove the "default" code from each loan you've rehabilitated. The negative payment history will remain, however.

Consolidation is worse for your credit score than rehabilitation. If you consolidate your defaulted student loans, you'll keep both the "default" code and the negative payment history on each loan. The trade-off is that you'll immediately be eligible for income driven repayment plans and federal student aid and you'll likely have a lower overall payment.

In the context of federal student loan cancellation, you have the **ABILITY TO BENEFIT** from the education or training being offered at an institution if you pass an approved ATB test or complete six credit hours towards a degree and at the time you took the test you had neither a high school diploma or GED equivalent.

You have an **ADVERSE CREDIT HISTORY** if you have had your wages garnished in the past five years, or have accounts that are over 90 days delinquent, or any unpaid collection accounts or if you:

- Received a bankruptcy discharge within the past five years;
- Voluntarily surrendered personal property or real property to avoid repossession or foreclosure within the past five years;
- Experienced a repossession within the past five years; or
- Defaulted on a loan, lease, or other contract.

An **ADMINISTRATIVE WAGE GARNISHMENT** allows the Department of Education to garnish your wages without having to get a judgment in court. Unless you agree to a higher amount, the Department can garnish the lesser of 15% of your DISPOSABLE PAY or the amount exceeding 30 times the federal minimum wage, which as of the day I wrote this is $7.25/hour.

CANCELLATION (or discharge) occurs when the Department of Education eliminates the balance you owe on a loan. When your loans are cancelled, you may be able to get back any money you paid on the loan, including money that was taken by wage garnishment, tax offset, and other collection efforts. If you're private lender offers cancellation, you'll have to contact it to learn more about what happens when the loan is cancelled.

CAPITALIZATION occurs when your unpaid interest is added to your loan's principal balance.

When you default on your federal student loans, **COLLECTION COSTS** of up to 18.5% (over 18.5% for your Perkins Loans) of your loan balance may be charged and added to your outstanding principal balance.

By getting a **CO-SIGNER RELEASE** you're causing a joint signer of a loan to be released from his liability on the loan.

You're in **DEFAULT** on your federal student loans when you haven't made a payment in over 270 days on a loan that was in repayment but had not been placed in deferment or forbearance. You're in default on your private student loans when you breach the contract you signed with your private student lender. Usually, a breach occurs when you haven't made a payment in 120 days on a loan that was in repayment but had not been placed in deferment or forbearance.

Under the PAYE and IBR plans, your **DISCRETIONARY INCOME** is the difference between your income and 150% of the poverty guideline for your family size and state of residence. Under the ICR plan, your discretionary income is the difference between your income and 100% of the poverty guideline for your family size and state of residence.

In the context of an administrative wage garnishment, your **DISPOSABLE PAY** is the amount of your pay remaining after deducting health insurance premiums and other amounts such as Social Security taxes and withholding taxes.

You can have your **FEDERAL BENEFITS OFFSET** (taken) to help repay a federal student loan you have defaulted on. The Department of Education can offset your Social Security benefits, your benefits under Part B of the Black Lung Act, and some Railroad Retirement benefits.

In the context of an AWG, you have a **FINANCIAL HARDSHIP** if garnishing 15% of your disposable income will create an undue financial hardship on you or your family.

Under the Teacher Loan Forgiveness program, state regulations control whether you're considered a **FULL-TIME EMPLOYEE**. If you work at more than one school, all qualifying employment is combined to determine if you're full time.

Your private student lender may issue a **GARNISHMENT** against your wage if it has a court ordered judgment to do so.

A **GUARANTY AGENCY** is a state or private nonprofit organization that administers FFEL Loans.

Your **LOAN HOLDER** is the entity holding your loan promissory note. That entity has the right to collect from you.

Your **LOAN SERVICER** is an entity that collects payments, answers your questions, and performs other administrative tasks for your loans on behalf of your lender.

Under the PAYE and IBR plans, you have a **PARTIAL FINANCIAL HARDSHIP** if your payment under the Standard plan would be greater than your payment under the IBR plan.

A **PARTIAL INTEREST SUBSIDY** under the PAYE plan means that for the first three years you're in the plan, the government will pay the interest accruing on your loans if your monthly plan payment doesn't cover all of your interest. Stated differently, if the amount you pay each month under the PAYE plan doesn't cover all the interest your loans are earning, the government will pay the leftover interest.

The **POVERTY GUIDELINES** are a version of the federal poverty measure that the Department of Health and Human Services issues each year in the Federal Register. Although the name's imprecise, the guidelines are often referred to as the "federal poverty level" . You can get the poverty guidelines for previous years at aspe.hhs.gov/poverty/index.cfm. Here's the 2015 poverty guideline.

Student loan **REHABILITATION** involves you bringing your loan out of default and removing the default notation from your credit report by making at least nine, timely payments of an agreed amount over a 10 month period. That's the rule for Direct Loans and FFEL Loans. For Perkins Loans, you must make your nine, timely payments in a nine month period.

Your federal student loans aren't subject to a **STATUTE OF LIMITATIONS**. As a result, the Department of Education can collect from you until you die. In contrast, your private student loans are subject to your state's statute of limitations for a breach of contract.

A **TAX OFFSET** occurs when the Department takes your income tax refund to help repay a federal student loan you have defaulted on.

In the context of your federal student loans, you're **TOTALLY AND PERMANENTLY DISABLED** if you're unable to work and earn money because of an illness or injury that's expected to result in death or has lasted or will last for a continuous period not less than 60 months. Your private student lender may adopt this standard of have its own standard for you to meet.

ACKNOWLEDGMENTS
#ITTOOKTHISVILLAGE

Thank you to each of you who helped make this happen. First, there's Spencer Boyer, Lisa Crooms, Okianer Christian Dark, Dannye Holley, Marcia Johnson, Homer C. La Rue, Kurt Schmoke, and April Walker. They not only trained me to be a lawyer, but they also showed me how to be a better human.

Second, there's Linda Aguilera, Omari Anderson, Alpha Bah, Boe Bowen, LaShea Borden, Khyla Craine, Willie Mae Duerson, Zondra Stovall Gaskins, Kourtney Gray, Laura Harding, Jill Hawkins, Lisa Caldwell Jones, Rachel Kelly, Pharra McDonald, Brian Morris, Solomon Morrow, Tarishawn Morton, Maryam Mujahid, , Susan Onyewuchi, Ramzi Oyathelemi, Duranté Partridge, Anthony Peterson, Shane Poole, Kevin Russell, Markita Samuel, Courtney Scrubbs, Cervana Shanklin, Leslie Simmons, Shanisha Smith, Rochelle Stanton, Soluto Uba, Bridgette Williams, and Tecee Winton. Thank you all for your contributions. You've made this book better with your suggestions and willingness to help.

Third, there's Wendell Sherk. You're the reason I got into student loan law. I don't know what caused you to take an interest in my career but I'm glad that you have. I look forward to continuing to learn from you. I hope that one day I can repay you for the kindness you've shown me.

Finally, there's Dominique. Your understanding and support are what I needed to make this book happen. Thank you.

BIBLIOGRAPHY
TATEESQ.COM/ABOUT

I'm one of the few attorneys in the United States practicing student loan law. I say practice because no man (or woman) is so much of an expert at anything — let alone student loan law — that he can afford not to practice at his craft daily. So that's what I do.

When I'm not helping clients with their student loans, I'm usually trying to find the world's best hamburger (Shake Shack is currently in pole position) or I'm playing basketball, watching HTGAWM, Being Mary Jane, Better Call Saul, and Hannibal, or doing some sort of DIY project around the house.